The GREAT Bool
DINOSAURS

Learn about the lives of the biggest and fiercest creatures of all time.

MICHAEL BENTON

www.alligatorbooks.co.uk

Published by
Alligator Books Limited
Gadd House, Arcadia Avenue
London N3 2JU

This volume is also published as four separate titles:
Discovering Dinosaurs Mighty Giants
Discovering Dinosaurs Flying Monsters
Discovering Dinosaurs Small & Scary
Discovering Dinosaurs Weird & Wonderful

Printed in China

10916

CONTENTS

EARTH'S LARGEST BEASTS

During their time on Earth, dinosaurs developed from small lizard-like creatures to the most spectacular group of reptiles that ever existed. Dinosaurs lived on Earth for 160 million years. When you consider that human beings have been around for less than 2 million years, you can see that the dinosaurs were around for far longer!

Meat-eating dinosaurs ranged from chicken-sized animals that ate insects to monsters the size of a bus that devoured animals their own size. Armoured dinosaurs, who had horns, spikes, and shields, were designed to put up a fierce fight against big predators. Yet the biggest dinosaurs were the long-necked plant-eaters. They remain the largest creatures to have ever walked on Earth.

In the beginning...

When the dinosaurs first appeared, the Earth consisted of one continent – a single landmass. The same dinosaurs existed everywhere. As the age of the dinosaurs went on, this landmass began to break up and drift apart into the five continents we have today.

Different kinds of dinosaurs developed in different continents. Towards the end of the dinosaur age, dinosaurs from Australia were different from those in North America, dinosaurs in Asia were different from those in Europe.

Disaster!

Then, suddenly they were gone. They all died out. For a long time, we did not know how or why. Now scientists believe that, about 65 million years ago, a huge meteorite or comet slammed into the Earth. It caused so much damage that few living things survived. The dinosaurs were killed, along with the flying reptiles – the pterosaurs – that existed with them. The big, sea-swimming reptiles of the time were also wiped out.

Discoveries

Only a few hundred dinosaurs have been discovered so far. Fossils and bones show how similar some of the smaller meat-eaters were to birds. This means that modern birds must have developed from them. **The Great Book of Dinosaurs** looks at these discoveries and many other well-known dinosaurs and pterosaurs of the dinosaur age. Each chapter focuses on a particular family or group of dinosaurs. You will see how they lived, what they ate and what special features they had that helped make them the most amazing creatures ever to have roamed the Earth.

FACTFILE: THE DINOSAUR AGE

- The Mesozoic Era lasted from 250 to 65 million years ago. Mesozoic means 'middle life'.

- The Cretaceous Period lasted from 150 to 65 million years ago. Cretaceous comes from the Latin *creta* ('chalk').

- The Jurassic Period lasted from 200 to 150 million years ago. It was named after the Jura Mountains, France.

- The Triassic Period lasted from 250 to 200 million years ago. Triassic means 'three-part'.

THE DINOSAUR AGE

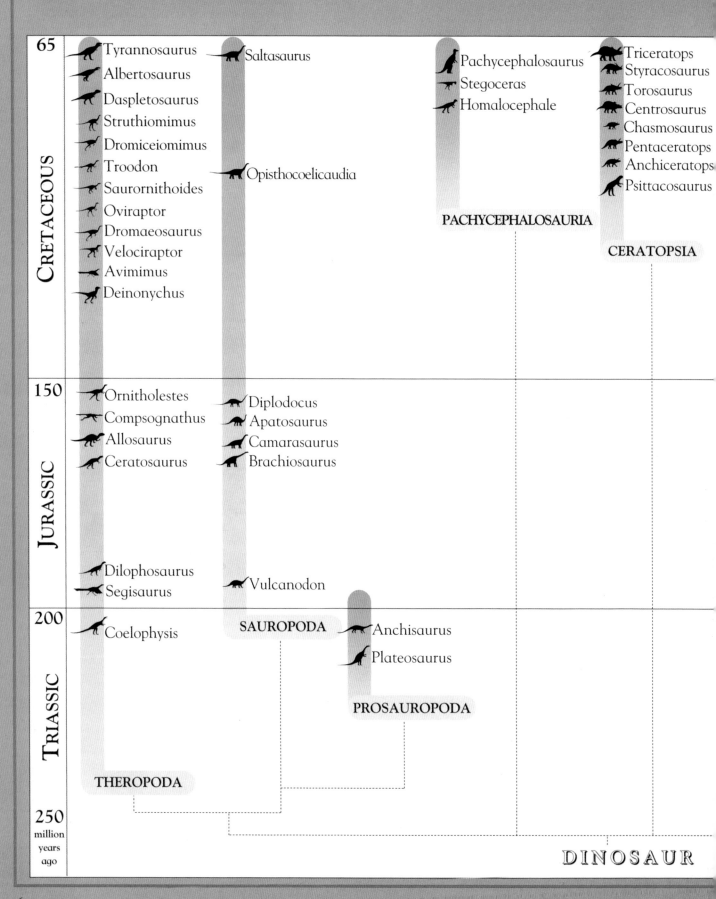

65

CRETACEOUS

Tyrannosaurus
Albertosaurus
Daspletosaurus
Struthiomimus
Dromiceiomimus
Troodon
Saurornithoides
Oviraptor
Dromaeosaurus
Velociraptor
Avimimus
Deinonychus

Saltasaurus

Opisthocoelicaudia

Pachycephalosaurus
Stegoceras
Homalocephale

Triceratops
Styracosaurus
Torosaurus
Centrosaurus
Chasmosaurus
Pentaceratops
Anchiceratops
Psittacosaurus

PACHYCEPHALOSAURIA

CERATOPSIA

150

JURASSIC

Ornitholestes
Compsognathus
Allosaurus
Ceratosaurus

Diplodocus
Apatosaurus
Camarasaurus
Brachiosaurus

Dilophosaurus
Segisaurus

Vulcanodon

200

TRIASSIC

Coelophysis

SAUROPODA

Anchisaurus
Plateosaurus

PROSAUROPODA

THEROPODA

250
million
years
ago

DINOSAUR

6

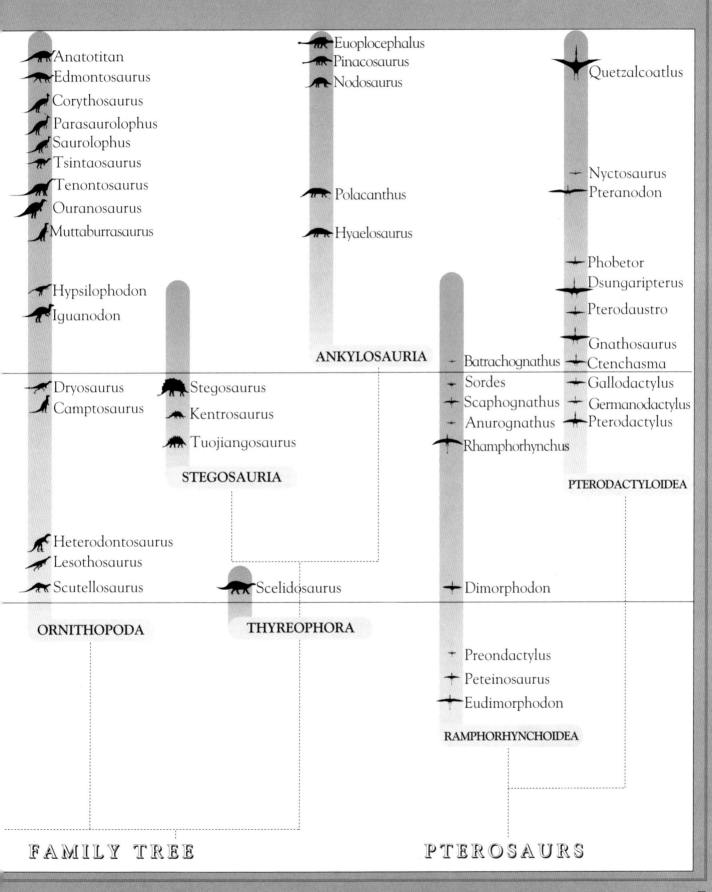

Anatotitan
Edmontosaurus
Corythosaurus
Parasaurolophus
Saurolophus
Tsintaosaurus
Tenontosaurus
Ouranosaurus
Muttaburrasaurus

Hypsilophodon
Iguanodon

Euoplocephalus
Pinacosaurus
Nodosaurus

Polacanthus

Hyaelosaurus

Quetzalcoatlus

Nyctosaurus
Pteranodon

Phobetor
Dsungaripterus
Pterodaustro

Gnathosaurus
Ctenchasma

ANKYLOSAURIA

Batrachognathus
Sordes
Scaphognathus
Anurognathus
Rhamphorhynchus

Gallodactylus
Germanodactylus
Pterodactylus

Dryosaurus
Camptosaurus

Stegosaurus
Kentrosaurus
Tuojiangosaurus

STEGOSAURIA

PTERODACTYLOIDEA

Heterodontosaurus
Lesothosaurus
Scutellosaurus

Scelidosaurus

Dimorphodon

ORNITHOPODA

THYREOPHORA

Preondactylus
Peteinosaurus
Eudimorphodon

RAMPHORHYNCHOIDEA

PEACEFUL GIANTS

Some of the largest dinosaurs were the vegetarian prosauropods and sauropods. The biggest sauropods were ten times the size of an elephant – the biggest land animal today.

BODY DEFENCES

The sauropods were one of the longest-living family of dinosaurs. A range of body defences helped them to survive the predators of the late Jurassic Period.

One of the first sauropods of the early Jurassic was *Vulcanodon* from Zimbabwe, Africa. It was smaller than most sauropods, but at 6.5 metres (21 feet) long, it was big enough to have straight pillar-like legs to support its body. Most of the toes ended in short 'hooves', except for the thumb claw, which was long and sharp. Perhaps this claw was used as a form of defence to fight off predators.

By the end of the dinosaur age in the late Cretaceous period, most of the sauropods were armoured with plates. These would have made it difficult for meat-eating dinosaurs to hunt them for food. *Saltasaurus,* from South America, had plates set in its skin. Large and small bony plates joined to form a strong chain mail. *Opisthocoelicaudia,* from China, had an unusually strong tail. This helped the dinosaur prop itself on two legs. It may have also been used as a defending 'weapon'.

HOW·DO I SAY THAT?

● **OPISTHOCOELICAUDIA**
OH-PISS-THO-SEE-LI-COW-DEE-AH

● **SALTASAURUS**
SAL-TA-SAW-RUS

● **VULCANODON**
VUL-KAY-NO-DON

Vulcanodon
Little is known about Vulcanodon, because only one incomplete skeleton has been found. The name means 'volcano tooth' – the first fossil was found close to some ancient volcanic lavas.

WHERE DID THEY LIVE?

- Opisthocoelicaudia
- Saltasaurus
- Vulcanodon

1   2   3

1. Opisthocoelicaudia 2. Saltasaurus 3. Vulcanodon

FACTFILE: SALTASAURUS

- Lived: 75 to 65 million years ago
- Group: Sauropoda
- Size: 12 metres (40 feet) long
- Weight: 30 tonnes
- Discovery: 1980, Salta Province, Argentina
- Diet: herbivore
- Special features: long neck, armour plates
- Name means 'Salta reptile'

Tail props
Opisthocoelicaudia *had a strong, stiff tail. This dinosaur used its tail as a prop. It could reach high into the trees by rocking back on the tail and lifting its front quarters off the ground.*

Plate armour
Saltosaurus *is famous for its armour plates. This was probably a good defence against predators.*

THE FIRST PLANT-EATERS

The true giants of the dinosaur age – the sauropods – evolved from medium-sized prosauropods such as *Plateosaurus*.

The first dinosaurs were human-sized, meat-eating reptiles. They appeared in the middle of the Triassic Period, around 230 million years ago. Then came the bigger, plant-eating 'early sauropods,' known as the prosauropods. Later, prosauropods evolved (developed over a long time) into the gigantic sauropods, such as *Diplodocus* and *Apatosaurus,* of the Jurassic Period.

The first large prosauropod was *Plateosaurus.* This dinosaur was 8 metres (26 feet) long. It was the largest land animal that had ever existed. Like all prosauropods, *Plateosaurus* walked on four legs, but it was light enough to stand easily and run on two legs. When it was standing, *Plateosaurus* used its huge hands, armed with claws, to pull tree branches to its mouth. Other large prosauropods included *Massospondylus* in South America and *Lufengosaurus* in Asia. Sauropods were heavier and four-footed. They were similar to *Plateosaurus* with their long, slender bodies, whiplike tails, enormously long necks, and thin, pencil-shaped teeth.

HOW DO I SAY THAT?

● PLATEOSAURUS
PLAT-EE-OH-SAW-RUS

Armed and dangerous!
Plateosaurus *had huge, powerful hands armed with long claws. The thumb was very strong and carried the largest claw.*

Plateosaurus

FACTFILE: PLATEOSAURUS

- Lived: 220 to 205 million years ago
- Group: Prosauropoda
- Size: 6-8 m (20-26 feet) long
- Weight: 4-6 tonnes
- Discovery: 1837, Germany
- Diet: herbivore
- Special features: powerful hands, walks on two or four legs
- Name means 'flat reptile'

Hands up!
As a plant-eater, Plateosaurus needed special hands that could support its weight, grasp tree branches, and fight off predators.

WHERE DID THEY LIVE?

● *Plateosaurus* ● Other prosauropods

Quick getaway
Plateosaurus fed close to the ground or high up in the trees. It moved around on all fours. When it was alarmed, it would rear up and run away on its hind legs.

CLASSIC GIANTS

The biggest dinosaurs of all time were the sauropods. *Diplodocus* **and** *Apatosaurus* **were the best known, with their long, snake-like necks.**

Diplodocus is the one of the longest sauropods that ever existed – it measured 27 metres (88 feet) from snout to tail. Why did sauropods have such long necks? It was probably to help them feed with less effort. Instead of wandering around, *Diplodocus* stood still and swept its head from side to side over a wide area of plants. When you weigh 30 tonnes, this takes much less energy than moving around all the time.

When fossils of *Apatosaurus* bones were first found, the skeleton had no head. It was suspected that the creature was the short-snouted *Camarasaurus*. Later study showed that it was *Apatosaurus* – a close relative of *Diplodocus* with a much longer head.

On the receiving end
Some scientists believe that the sauropods used their enormously long tails to hit their enemies.

HOW DO I SAY THAT?

⬤ **APATOSAURUS**
AH-<u>PAT</u>-OH-<u>SAW</u>-RUS
⬤ **DIPLODOCUS**
DIP-<u>LOD</u>-O-<u>KUS</u>

1. Apatosaurus 2. Diplodocus

FACTFILE: APATOSAURUS

- Lived: 160 to 150 million years ago
- Group: Sauropoda
- Size: 21 m (70 feet) long
- Weight: 30 tonnes
- Discovery: 1877, Colorado, U.S.A.
- Diet: herbivore
- Special features: long neck, heavy body
- Name means: 'deceptive reptile'

Vegetarian life

Plant-eating dinosaurs had to eat a lot to stay healthy. Grass did not appear on Earth until after the dinosaurs had become extinct. Apatosaurus might have fed on tough plants called ferns. It stripped the leaves off with its blunt, pencil-like teeth. Apatosaurus probably had stones inside its stomach to help grind up the plants.

WHERE DID THEY LIVE?

Apatosaurus and Diplodocus

THE BIGGEST EVER?

Most records of huge dinosaurs are based on limited fossil evidence – a giant leg bone or other parts of a monster skeleton. But few people doubt the enormity of *Brachiosaurus*.

Complete skeletons of *Brachiosaurus* were found in Tanzania, Africa, and they are huge. One of the skeletons is on display at the Humboldt Museum in Berlin, Germany, where it towers four floors high. With its long neck and enormous front legs, *Brachiosaurus* reached high above any other dinosaur to crop leaves from the tallest trees.

Camarasaurus was much smaller than *Brachiosaurus*. At 18 metres (60 feet) long, however, it was still the size of six elephants! The head of *Camarasaurus* had a short snout. The jaws were lined with sharp teeth to chew on tough vegetation. As with *Brachiosaurus* and all the giant, plant-eating dinosaurs, *Camarasaurus* had front legs that were shorter than the back legs. Its feet were heavily padded – to absorb the shock of impact from the creature's huge weight on the ground.

HOW DO I SAY THAT?

BRACHIOSAURUS
BRAK-EE-OH-SAW-RUS

CAMARASAURUS
KAM-AH-RA-SAW-RUS

Head first
Brachiosaurus *is the tallest dinosaur known from a complete skeleton. For such a mountain of flesh and bone, the head of this creature might seem strangely small.*

Sharp teeth
Herbivore Brachiosaurus had sharp, peglike teeth for raking leaves from branches.

1. Camarasaurus 2. Brachiosaurus

FACTFILE: BRACHIOSAURUS

- Lived: 160 to 150 million years ago
- Group: Sauropoda
- Size: 22.5 m (73 feet) long, 12 m (40 feet) tall
- Weight: 50 tonnes
- Discovery: 1900, Colorado, U.S.A.
- Diet: herbivore
- Special features: the tallest dinosaur, crest over eyes
- Name means: 'arm reptile'

WHERE DID THEY LIVE?

- *Brachiosaurus* and *Camarasaurus*
- *Brachiosaurus*

Short differences
Camarasaurus *was smaller than Brachiosaurus.*
It had a shorter neck and front legs.

AMAZING ANCHISAURUS

Among the first small plant-eating dinosaurs to appear on Earth were the prosauropods from the late Triassic Period.

The first prosauropods were small reptiles, even though their later relatives – sauropods like *Apatosaurus* and *Diplodocus* – were giants. One of the smallest prosauropods was *Anchisaurus*. It was the height of a terrier dog but much longer. Fossils of *Anchisaurus* were actually the first dinosaur remains to be found in North America. *Anchisaurus* was lightly built and agile enough to escape quickly from the predatory dinosaurs of its day.

Head and hands
Anchisaurus had a small head and a long neck. Its teeth were small and pencil-shaped, so it probably fed on leaves from bushes and small trees. Anchisaurus had five toes on each foot, and its broad thumb was armed with a large claw that was used to grasp plants.

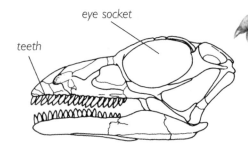

eye socket

teeth

Skull
Anchisaurus had a very large eye socket. Its teeth were coarsely serrated and packed tightly together for grinding up tough plants.

HOW DO I SAY THAT?

● ANCHISAURUS
AN-KIH-SAW-RUS

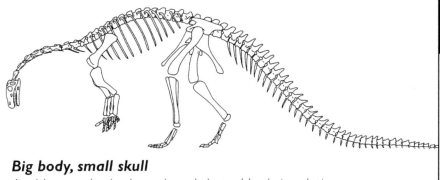

Big body, small skull

Anchisaurus *had a large, barrel-shaped body in relation to the size of its tiny skull. This is similar to most plant-eating dinosaurs. Plant-eaters need a bigger stomach to digest raw plant food than meat-eating animals.*

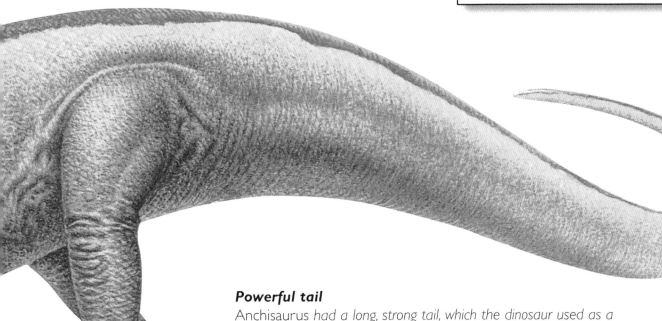

Powerful tail

Anchisaurus *had a long, strong tail, which the dinosaur used as a counterbalance when it ran on its back legs. The tail had powerful muscles – this is shown by the high position of the spine and the deep, riblike bones.* Anchisaurus *may have whipped its tail from side-to-side to scare predators.*

Versatile mover

Powerful legs and strong arms allowed Anchisaurus *to walk on all fours. To break into a run, the dinosaur would only have used its back legs.*

Anchisaurus

WHERE DID THEY LIVE?

● Anchisaurus

BUILT FOR STRENGTH

When you look at a sauropod's skeleton, you can see that it is built for strength. The long neck and tail worked like the boom on a crane. In a large sauropod, the neck must have weighed about four tonnes, so it had to be strong. Powerful muscles and ligaments ran down the top of the neck. These could shorten to lift the neck up. The long, whiplike tail could be raised and swung rapidly from side to side, probably to whack predators.

THE PROSAUROPODS & SAUROPODS:

- *Anchisaurus*
- *Apatosaurus*
- *Brachiosaurus*
- *Camarasaurus*
- *Diplodocus*
- *Opisthocoelicaudia*
- *Plateosaurus*
- *Saltasaurus*
- *Vulcanodon*

Underwater swimmers?

This picture shows Brachiosaurus *standing in deep water. Scientists used to think that sauropods lived underwater. In the same way that your body floats in water, scientists believed that water would have helped support the huge weight of these dinosaurs. Sauropods could have floated in lakes, and fed on plants around the lake edge. The problem with this theory is that these dinosaurs could not have breathed in deep water. Their lungs would have been about 5 metres (16 feet) below the surface. At that depth, the water pressure would have squashed their lungs.*

Brachiosaurus

DINO DICTIONARY

- **Paleontologist:** a scientist who studies fossils
- **Skeleton:** the bony framework that supports the body
- **Vertebra:** a small bone of the backbone

Wonder of the world

A complete skeleton of Brachiosaurus has been put together from fossils collected in Africa around 1912. It can be seen in the Humboldt Museum in Berlin, Germany. The huge, powerful neck towers high into the exhibit hall, and people can walk under the dinosaur's belly.

Big bones

Sauropods such as Brachiosaurus had massive hands and feet to support their huge weight. The bones are enormous — each toe bone is as big as your thigh bone!

hand bones ———————

——————— hind foot bones

GIANT REPTILES

Why were some dinosaurs so big? Large animals have a lot of advantages. A big carnivore can kill almost anything, so it will never go hungry. A huge herbivore can be so big that no meat-eater can attack it – think of a lion trying to eat an elephant. Big animals can cover long distances in search of food. However, large animals have to eat a lot. Their weight can put a strain on their bones, causing health problems, such as arthritis.

The longest dinosaur known was *Diplodocus*. Its skeleton measured 27 metres (88 feet) in length. Giants like *Diplodocus* weighed about 50 tonnes. It had four legs, so each leg had to support more than 10 tonnes. Its backbone was like the flat surface of a bridge, slung between the hip girdle and the shoulder girdle. It needed strong muscles and ligaments just to support its huge weight. Giant dinosaurs could not move fast. If *Diplodocus* tried to gallop, it would have broken its legs.

DINO DICTIONARY

- **Carnivore:** an animal that feeds on meat and flesh
- **Herbivore:** an animal that feeds on plants

Tailing off
The sauropod tail was long and whip-like. It was made up of many very small vertebrae.

Streamlined back
Sauropods had long spines on each vertebra. These spines held powerful muscles.

Strong tails
Spines above and below the tail vertebrae (segments of the backbone) helped the muscles whip the tail up and down and from side to side.

Upright legs
The legs and feet of sauropods were thick, short and sturdy to support their vast weight.

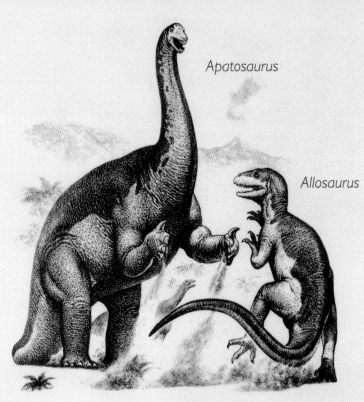

Apatosaurus

Allosaurus

Clawed-up sauropods

Paleontologists have been puzzled by the big thumb claws of the sauropods. It is thought that they were used to fight off predators. Apatosaurus may have reared up and threatened fearsome flesh-eaters such as Allosaurus.

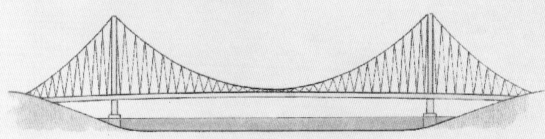

Giant bridges

Sauropods are built like suspension bridges. A suspension bridge uses massive steel cables to hold up the flat road surface over which cars and people cross. In a sauropod, the backbone, long neck, and tail, were held up by huge cable-like muscles and tendons that stretched along the back.

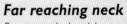

Diplodocus

Far reaching neck

Sauropods had long necks. Powerful muscles were needed to move the head and neck around.

FEARSOME HUNTERS

With their biting jaws and vicious claws, the theropods were a ferocious family of meat-eating predators. *T-rex* may be the most well-known monster, but small, vulture-like ornithomimids were just as scary.

MEAT-EATERS

***Tyrannosaurus* was a fearsome hunter, but small predatory theropods were just as fierce.**

The first dinosaurs were small, fast-running, meat-eating theropods. Theropods ('beast feet') walked on two back legs and had sharp claws on their hands and bird-like feet. They used their hands to grab their prey, and possibly to carry pieces of meat to devour later.

Coelophysis was one of the earliest theropods. *Ornitholestes* and *Compsognathus* came later in the late Jurassic Period. All three reptiles had similar features and habits. They had slender bodies, long flexible necks, powerful legs, sharp teeth and strong clawed hands. Groups of *Coelophysis* fossils were found in North America. This suggests that these dinosaurs may have hunted in packs, like wolves today. Since the fossils were found in a group, these dinosaurs may have died together in a drought.

1. *Compsognathus* 2. *Ornitholestes*
3. *Coelophysis*

HOW DO I SAY THAT?

⬤ **COELOPHYSIS**
SEEL-OH-FY-SIS

⬤ **COMPSOGNATHUS**
KOMP-SOG-NAY-THUS

⬤ **ORNITHOLESTES**
OR-NITH-OH-LESS-TEEZ

Sharp-toothed hunter
Ornitholestes had sharp teeth that pointed inward, trapping prey in its mouth. This dinosaur may have snatched flesh from prey that had been killed by larger dinosaurs.

FACTFILE: COELOPHYSIS

- Lived: 230 to 220 million years ago
- Group: Theropoda
- Size: 3 m (10 feet) long, 1.5 m (5 feet) tall
- Weight: 45 kg (100 pounds)
- Discovery: 1881, New Mexico, U.S.A.
- Diet: carnivore
- Special features: slender body, long tail
- Name means: 'hollow form'

Slim and ferocious
Coelophysis *was a small but merciless predator. A skeleton of a younger dinosaur was found in the stomach of an adult.*

Small and speedy
Compsognathus *was one of the smallest dinosaurs. It was about as big as a cat. Compsognathus was an active predator; it chased small prey, such as lizards and insects. Its small hands were unusual for dinosaurs of the time.*

WHERE DID THEY LIVE?
- Coelophysis and Ornitholestes
- Compsognathus

SMALL HUNTERS

Every part of the skeleton of a small theropod was designed for quick movement and effective hunting. The skull was narrow and the jaws were powerful. The neck was long and flexible to allow the dinosaur to thrust and dive its head like a snake. The hands were strong, so predators could wrestle their prey to the ground. The legs were long, agile and powerful, and designed for running. The whiplike tail provided balance when these predators pursued their fast-moving prey.

Light headed
Like Compsognathus, Coelophysis *had a hollow skull and long jaws lined with serrated teeth.*

Compsognathus

The first theropods
Coelophysis *was one of the earliest theropods. It had many features that were similar to other small theropods. It had long arms and relatively short legs, so it could rest on all fours when it fed.*

Coelophysis

Strong hands
Coelophysis *had fingers on each hand, so it could grasp its prey effectively.*

Nimble predator
Compsognathus *was one of the smallest dinosaurs that ever lived. It had a slender, pointed snout so it could dig deep inside the animal to strip off the meat.*

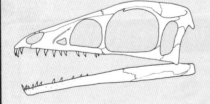

Compsognathus *skull*
This hollow skull was typical of a predator that caught small, fast-moving animals, such as lizards and insects.

Clawed hands
Long-fingered hands were better at grasping prey, so it is unusual for a small predator like Compsognathus to have short hands with claws.

Running legs
Compsognathus *had long, slender legs typical of small, fast-moving dinosaurs. This dinosaur had three long, forward-pointing toes on each foot, as well as a backward-pointing fourth toe.*

Fingers and thumbs

Ornitholestes *had long hands with powerful fingers. It may have used them to control its struggling prey. The dinosaur had two long fingers and a short first finger. It probably gripped its prey, using the short finger like a thumb.*

Big biter

Ornitholestes *had a heavier skull than some of its relatives. It had a short, compact snout and more robust teeth, so it is likely* Ornitholestes *had a stronger bite than* Compsognathus *and* Coelophysis.

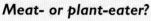

Ornitholestes

Balancing act

The long tails of these dinosaurs stuck out straight behind them and provided a counterbalance as they ran.

Meat- or plant-eater?

Some small theropods, such as the ornithomimids like Struthiomimus, *had no teeth in their mouths. These dinosaurs may have fed on plants – grasping branches in their strong fingers and tearing off the leaves with their jaws. However, this would have been an unusual diet for a theropod – most were meat-eating predators. Scientists have not found clear evidence to prove whether they were solely meat- or plant-eaters. They may have lived on both animal flesh and vegetation.*

JURASSIC KILLERS

Predators had huge heads, powerful jaws, and ferocious teeth – which they used to sink into the flesh of other dinosaurs they hunted.

The dinosaur age is often linked to the word 'Jurassic'. This refers to the period of time when large, meat-eating theropods appeared – about 195 million years ago. The best-known Jurassic theropod was *Allosaurus*. Its powerful teeth could tear the flesh of its prey into large chunks. *Ceratosaurus* lived at the same time as *Allosaurus*, but it was half the size and fed on much smaller prey. *Ceratosaurus*, meaning 'horned reptile', had odd-looking bumps on its skull that probably made it look more frightening. *Dilophosaurus* lived earlier in the Jurassic Period. It is famous for a pair of crests on the top of its head. The crests looked like two halves of a dinner plate set up on their ends.

1 2 3

1. Ceratosaurus 2. Dilophosaurus
3. Allosaurus

Dilophosaurus

Ceratosaurus

HOW DO I SAY THAT?

● **ALLOSAURUS**
AL-OH-<u>SAW</u>-RUS

● **CERATOSAURUS**
SEE-<u>RAT</u>-OH-<u>SAW</u>-RUS

● **DILOPHOSAURUS**
DIE-<u>LOW</u>-FOE-<u>SAW</u>-RUS

WHERE DID THEY LIVE?

● *Allosaurus, Ceratosaurus* and *Dilophosaurus*

FACTFILE: ALLOSAURUS

Lived: 160 to 150 million years ago

Group: Theropoda

Size: 12 m (40 feet) long

Weight: 4 to 5 tonnes

Discovery: 1877, Colorado, U.S.A.

Diet: carnivore

Special features: massive skull, powerful hands

Name means: 'other reptile'

Fossil find

When 5,000 Allosaurus bones were found in a quarry in Utah, USA, this large meat-eater became the best-known Jurassic theropod. It had sharp teeth and strong hands, each with three clawed fingers. It killed its prey by clamping its jaws around the animal's neck.

Allosaurus

THE SLASHERS

The dromaeosaurids may have been human-sized dinosaurs, but their sickle-shaped claw on the second toe of each foot made them ferocious monsters.

The first dromaeosaurid fossils were found about 100 years ago, but scientists could not tell what these dinosaurs looked like because the fossils were incomplete. Then, in 1964, full skeletons of *Deinonychus* were found in North America. *Deinonychus* had good eyesight and a large head, so it probably had a relatively big brain for a dinosaur. It had long legs and arms, and a stiff tail for balance, so it may have been a fast runner. *Velociraptor* can be distinguished from *Deinonychus* and *Dromaeosaurus* by its low, narrow head. The differences in head shape may reflect differences in the diets of these dinosaurs.

The one thing that these dinosaurs had in common was their similarity to birds. Their bones were bird-like, their joints were bird-like and their lifestyle suggested they were warm-blooded – just like birds. We now think that they were closely related to the ancestors of birds, and were probably covered in feathers.

WHERE DID THEY LIVE?

- Deinonychus
- Dromaeosaurus
- Velociraptor

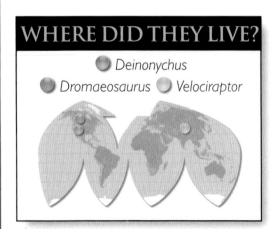

Dromaeosaurus
Little is known about Dromaesosaurus, *the first dromaeosaurid. Only parts of the skull and a few leg bones were found in 1914. Scientists put the rest of the skeleton together when complete fossils of* Deinonychus *were found.*

Big mouth

The jaws of Deinonychus were lined with many backward-pointing teeth. Prey could not escape once it was in the dinosaur's teeth. If it struggled, the animal just moved further down the dinosaur's throat.

FACTFILE: DEINONYCHUS

- Lived: 110 to 100 million years ago
- Group: Theropoda
- Size: 3 m (10 feet) long, 1.5 m (5 feet) tall
- Weight: 75 kg (165 pounds)
- Discovery: 1964, Montana, U.S.A.
- Diet: carnivore
- Special features: slashing claw, stiff tail
- Name means: 'terrible claw'

Caught in the act

Velociraptor was an extremely efficient predator – better than many larger predators. A fossil from Mongolia shows a Velociraptor locked in a fight with a horned dinosaur called Protoceratops. Velociraptor is shown grasping the head shield of Protoceratops. This suggests that these dinosaurs probably died together in a freak sandstorm. The remains of Velociraptor were not found with Dromaeosaurus and Deinonychus. It is unlikely that they all lived together as shown in this picture.

1. Dromaeosaurus
2. Velociraptor
3. Deinonychus

HOW DO I SAY THAT?

- **DEINONYCHUS**
  DINE-ON-IKE-US
- **DROMAEOSAURUS**
  DROM-AY-OH-SAW-RUS
- **VELOCIRAPTOR**
  VEL-OSS-IH-RAP-TOR

33

ANATOMY OF A KILLER

Deinonychus was a perfect hunter. Every part of its body – from the tip of its snout to the end of its tail – was designed for speed and ferocity. But the dinosaur's key weapon was the slashing claw on each foot. This required more skill than that shown by any other dinosaur. *Deinonychus* may have been good at keeping balance and probably had excellent eyesight as well. It could stand on one leg, slash its victim with the other claw, land back on both feet, and twist around, ready to strike again.

Claw position for running

Claw movement for attacking

Vicious weapon
Instead of using its teeth like a typical predator, Deinonychus' main weapons were its legs and its huge claws. When Deinonychus ran, it held its slashing foot upright. However, it could swing its foot through more than 180 degrees to attack its prey.

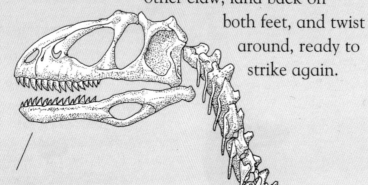

Head
The high skull shows that Deinonychus had powerful jaw muscles.

Deinonychus

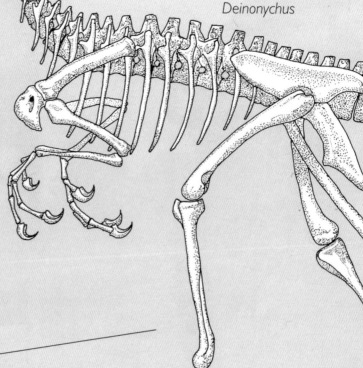

Powerful arms
Deinonychus had strong arms with long fingers for grasping its prey.

Fast legs
Deinonychus had strong back legs for running and a stiff tail that acted like a balancing rod.

Hunting

It is likely that *Deinonychus* hunted large prey in a pack and smaller prey on its own (right). A fossil skeleton of *Tenontosaurus* – a dinosaur ten times bigger than *Deinonychus* – was discovered surrounded by several *Deinonychus*. So five or six *Deinonychus* may have attacked a larger animal (as shown below) – like a pack of wild dogs do today.

1. *Deinonychus* runs up fast from behind as it hunts a smaller dinosaur.

2. *Deinonychus* leaps on the back of its prey, and sinks its teeth into the soft neck muscles.

Flexible and rigid

Deinonychus had a short, strong back. This allowed it to twist and turn effectively when it hunted. Its tail consisted of fine, bony rods that made it stiff.

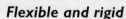

3. The killing claw rips the victim's belly open, and *Deinonychus* begins its feast.

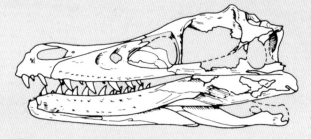

Similar relative

Velociraptor was a relative of *Deinonychus*, but it had a much flatter skull. Despite the differences in their skulls, the skeletons of the two dinosaurs are very similar, although *Velociraptor* was half the size of *Deinonychus*. This fossilized skull is slightly crushed – you can see how some of the bones do not fit exactly.

DINO DICTIONARY

Prey: an animal that is hunted

Predator: a flesh-eating hunter

Carcass: the dead body of an animal

Skull: the bones of the head

BIG-EYED RUNNERS

Dinosaurs had very small brains in relation to the size of their bodies. But the troodontids were amongst the dinosaurs with the largest brains.

Troodontids like *Saurornithoides* and *Troodon* were fast-moving, lightly built theropods. Their bodies were similar to the ornithomimids. They had ostrich-like necks, small heads, long legs and tails. But troodontids had stronger hands and feet, with huge slashing claws.

For their body size, troodontids had brains that were bigger than the normal size for dinosaurs. This could mean they may have been the most intelligent! By filling a fossil skull with dry lentils, then pouring them into a measuring jug, scientists have figured out the size of many dinosaurs' brains.

WHERE DID THEY LIVE?

● *Saurornithoides* ● *Troodon*

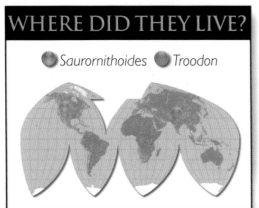

Knifelike claws
Saurornithoides used the claws on its feet to kill its prey. It grabbed small mammals and lizards, and held them tight while tearing the flesh with its teeth. This dinosaur had to rely on its hands and feet, because its teeth were very small and could not have been used to kill its prey.

FACTFILE: SAURORNITHOIDES

- Lived: 85 to 70 million years ago
- Group: Theropoda
- Size: 2 m (6 1/2 feet) long
- Weight: 50 kg (110 pounds)
- Discovery: 1923, Mongolia
- Diet: carnivore
- Special features: big brain, beady eyes
- Name means: 'birdlike reptile'

1. Troodon   2. Saurornithoides

Big, beady eyes

Troodon *had big, beady eyes set high up on the snout, so it could look forward as well as sideways. Most dinosaurs had their eyes set on the side of their heads like a horse, so each eye saw a different scene. Troodontids may have been able to see in three dimensions like we can.*

HOW DO I SAY THAT?

SAURORNITHOIDES
SAWR-OR-NITH-OIDE-EEZ
TROODON
TROO-DON

PATTERNS & FEATHERS

Small dinosaurs may have been just as successful at hunting prey as large dinosaurs.

It is difficult to know how dinosaurs looked, because fossils cannot tell us about the colour of their skin. Many reptiles today, such as lizards and snakes, have colourful skin patterns. Some dinosaurs might have been the same. Colourful skin patterns would have helped to ward off bigger predators. *Segisaurus* – a small theropod and a relative of *Coelophysis* – is shown here with colourful body stripes. Another intriguing theropod was *Avimimus*. Its skeleton interested scientists because of its mixture of bird-like and dinosaur features. The fossil of *Avimimus* showed that the dinosaur had a ridge along the arm bones. Birds have a similar structure to fix their feathers in place. As a result, scientists believe that many dinosaurs were feathered.

Segisaurus
This little hunter had short arms and three fingers on each hand. It had long, powerful legs, so it may have been a fast-mover.

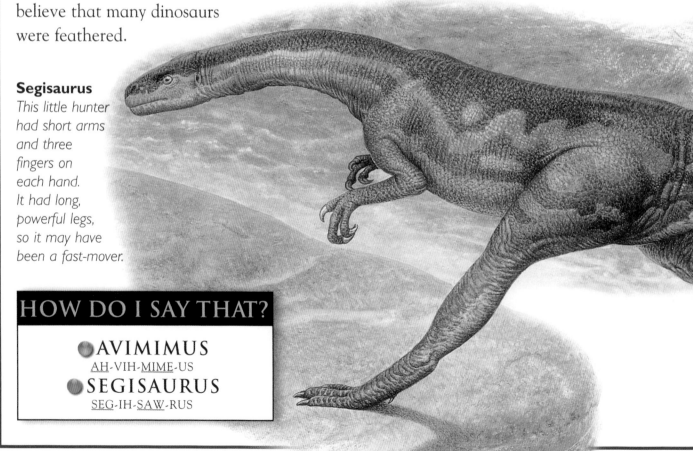

HOW DO I SAY THAT?

⬤ **AVIMIMUS**
AH-VIH-MIME-US

⬤ **SEGISAURUS**
SEG-IH-SAW-RUS

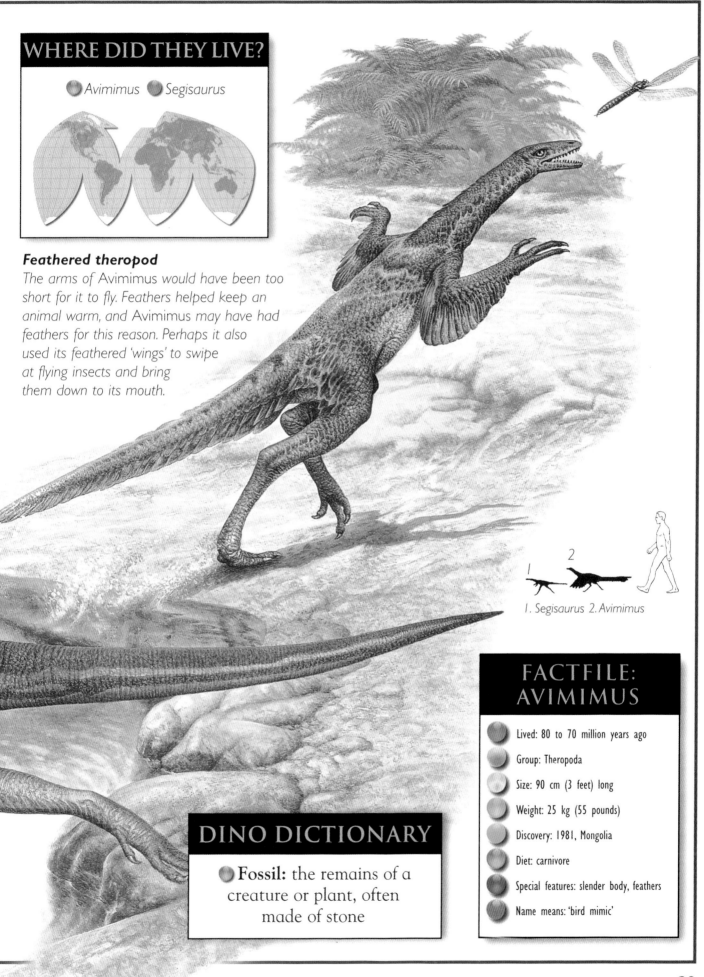

Feathered theropod

The arms of Avimimus would have been too short for it to fly. Feathers helped keep an animal warm, and Avimimus may have had feathers for this reason. Perhaps it also used its feathered 'wings' to swipe at flying insects and bring them down to its mouth.

1. Segisaurus 2. Avimimus

FACTFILE: AVIMIMUS

● Lived: 80 to 70 million years ago

● Group: Theropoda

● Size: 90 cm (3 feet) long

● Weight: 25 kg (55 pounds)

● Discovery: 1981, Mongolia

● Diet: carnivore

● Special features: slender body, feathers

● Name means: 'bird mimic'

DINO DICTIONARY

● **Fossil:** the remains of a creature or plant, often made of stone

39

THE OSTRICH DINOSAURS

Ornithomimids were fast-running, meat-eating hunters but, strangely enough, they had no teeth.

Why didn't the ornithomimids have teeth? They may have eaten food, such as insects and eggs, for which teeth were not needed. It is also likely that the ornithomimids had sharp-edged beaks, like modern eagles and vultures. These beaks were used to kill prey by tearing up the flesh.

Struthiomimus
With its speedy legs and strong hands, Struthiomimus may have hunted insects, such as dragonflies. Struthiomimus was probably too big an animal to survive on just insects. It is likely it also hunted lizards and other small animals.

Coming to get you!
Ostrich dinosaurs had long, strong fingers with claws to grab small animals and tear them apart.

HOW DO I SAY THAT?

● **DROMICEIOMIMUS**
DROM-IK-AY-OH-MIME-US
● **OVIRAPTOR**
OVE-IH-RAP-TOR
● **STRUTHIOMIMUS**
STROOTH-EE-OH-MIME-US

1. Oviraptor
2. Struthiomimus
3. Dromiceiomimus

Dromiceiomimus and Struthiomimus
Oviraptor

Strange head

Oviraptor *had an unusual skull with a hornlike structure over its snout. The purpose of this nose horn is not known.*

Dromiceiomimus

This dinosaur was a close relative of Struthiomimus *but it had a shorter back and more slender legs. When Dromiceiomimus chased its prey, it tucked up its arms and stuck its tail out stiffly to act as a counterbalance.*

Run like a horse

Ornithomimids appeared in the late Cretaceous Period. They had long, slender back legs like modern ostriches. They may have run at speeds of 50 km/h (31 mph) – as fast as a race horse.

Egg thief?

Although Oviraptor was not a true ornithomimid, it was feathered just like a bird. Oviraptor ('egg thief') was named when the first fossils were found near nests in Mongolia. Recent studies have shown that these nests actually belonged to Oviraptor. The dinosaur was looking after its own eggs, not stealing them!

FACTFILE: STRUTHIOMIMUS

Lived: 75 to 65 million years ago

Group: Theropoda

Size: 3-4 m (10-13 feet) long

Weight: 100 kg (220 pounds)

Discovery: 1917, Alberta, Canada

Diet: carnivore

Special features: long powerful legs, toothless jaws

Name means: 'ostrich mimic'

LIVING DINOSAURS?

UP CLOSE

Some small dinosaurs have skeletons almost identical to *Archaeopteryx* – the oldest known bird. *Archaeopteryx* was one of the most famous fossil finds. It showed that dinosaur ancestors of birds developed the ability to fly. *Archaeopteryx* fossils date from the late Jurassic Period and were found in Germany. The fossils clearly show the skeleton and delicate outlines of the feathers, which were preserved as soft imprints in the ancient mud.

When the first *Archaeopteryx* fossil was found in 1861, it provided the 'missing link' in the story of evolution between reptiles and birds. Paleontologists had always thought that birds evolved from reptiles. They pointed to clues, such as the scales on a bird's legs. But the *Archaeopteryx* discovery provided much stronger evidence. *Archaeopteryx* was a bird with feathers and wings, but it also had some dinosaur features, such as teeth, claws, and a long, bony tail. In fact, the skeleton of *Archaeopteryx* is remarkably similar to the little theropod – *Compsognathus*.

DINO DICTIONARY

- **Paleontologist:** a scientist who studies fossils
- **Evolution:** the development of animals over a very long time

Archaeopteryx *fossil*
The first bird had wings that were identical in structure to the wings of a modern bird. The first bird had long, fingerlike feathers. The wing muscles would not have been as strong as a modern bird, but the flying action was probably the same.

Skull comparison
The teeth and eye sockets in an Archaeopteryx skull are reptilian features and are similar to those of the dinosaur Compsognathus.

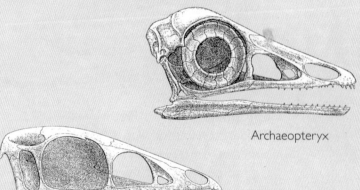

Archaeopteryx

Compsognathus

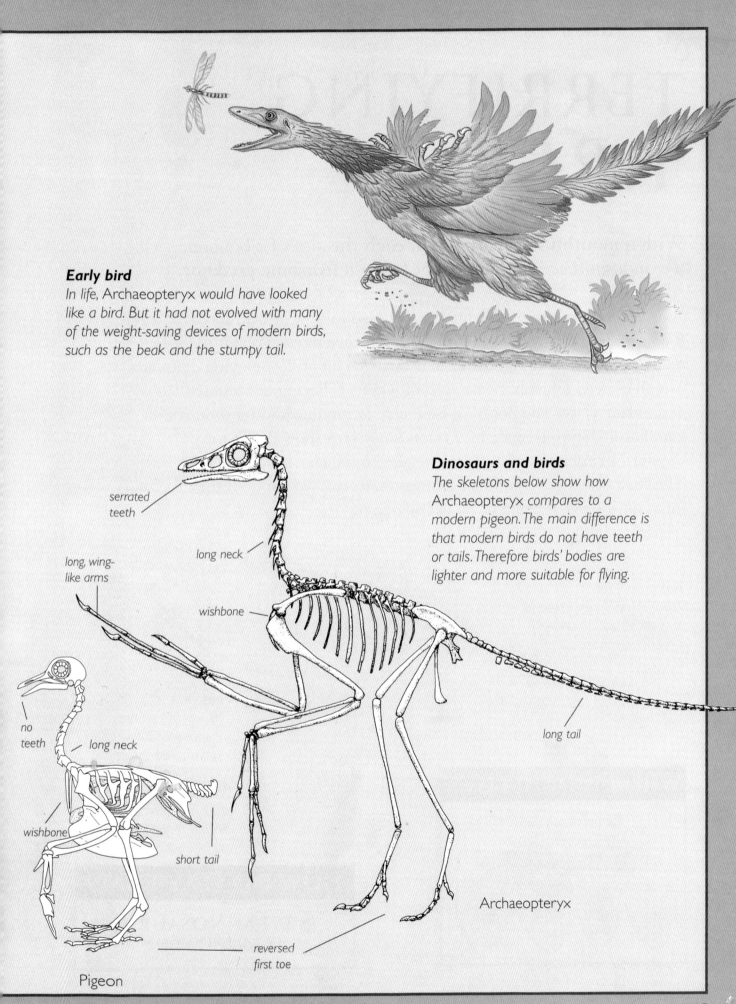

Early bird

In life, Archaeopteryx would have looked like a bird. But it had not evolved with many of the weight-saving devices of modern birds, such as the beak and the stumpy tail.

serrated teeth

long neck

long, wing-like arms

wishbone

Dinosaurs and birds

The skeletons below show how Archaeopteryx compares to a modern pigeon. The main difference is that modern birds do not have teeth or tails. Therefore birds' bodies are lighter and more suitable for flying.

long tail

no teeth

long neck

wishbone

short tail

reversed first toe

Archaeopteryx

Pigeon

TERRIFYING T. REX

With a mouthful of sharp teeth, each the size of a banana, *Tyrannosaurus rex* is famous for being a fearsome predator.

Was *Tyrannosaurus rex* a hunter that chased its prey at high speed, or was it a meat-eating scavenger? Fossil footprints give us clues about the speed and weight of a dinosaur. *T. rex* may have fed off of slow-moving dinosaurs as well as dead animals. Some paleontologists believe that because *T. rex* was so heavy, it would not have been able to run much faster than you can. Fossil footprints made by *Tyrannosaurus rex* show that it ran around 24 km/h (15 mph). *T. rex* weighed as much as two elephants. This load would have put a lot of stress on its two leg bones. If the dinosaur tripped, it could never get up again.

Tail

When it ran, T. rex raised its tail high off the ground as a counterbalance.

Skull

T. rex had a huge head with deep, powerful jaws.

Feet

T. rex stood on two massive feet. It had a large claw at the end of each of its toes. A tiny fourth toe stuck out behind, but it did not reach the ground.

WHERE DID THEY LIVE?

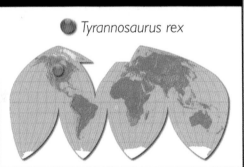

● *Tyrannosaurus rex*

HOW DO I SAY THAT?

 TYRANNOSAURUS
TIE-RAN-OH-SAW-RUS

FACTFILE: TYRANNOSAURUS

- Lived: 75 to 65 million years ago
- Group: Theropoda
- Size: 14 m (46 feet) long, 6 m (20 feet) tall
- Weight: 6-7 tonnes
- Discovery: 1902, Montana, U.S.A.
- Diet: carnivore
- Special features: huge teeth, tiny arms
- Name means 'tyrant reptile'

Tyrannosaurus rex

Monster munch

T. rex *was twice as tall as an elephant and could have picked you up in its jaws. It fed by holding down prey with one foot, and tearing the flesh into strips with its strong jaws. It is hard to see how* T. rex *used its tiny arms. They did not even reach its mouth!*

TYRANT HUNTERS

Tyrannosaurids, such as *Albertosaurus* and *Daspletosaurus*, were relatives of *T. rex*. Since they were smaller, they moved much faster than their big relatives.

Like *T. rex*, *Albertosaurus* had only two fingers on its short arms. But *Albertosaurus* was probably more of an active hunter than *T. rex*. It would have killed its prey either by biting a lump of flesh from the neck, or by a powerful kick with its foot.

Daspletosaurus lived at the same time as *Albertosaurus*. Scientists cannot explain how two different tyrannosaurids were able to live without competing for the same food. *Daspletosaurus* had a heavier head and larger teeth than *Albertosaurus*, so perhaps it hunted different animals. Both were big enough to fight with big plant-eaters, such as the duckbill hadrosaurs.

Powerful jaws
Daspletosaurus may have killed its prey by snapping its jaws into the flanks of an animal, and leaving it to bleed to death.

HOW DO I SAY THAT?

● **ALBERTOSAURUS**
AL-BERT-OH-SAW-RUS

● **DASPLETOSAURUS**
DASS-PLEET-OH-SAW-RUS

1. Daspletosaurus 2. Albertosaurus

Albertosaurus   Daspletosaurus

Moving in on the kill
Like many meat-eating animals today, Albertosaurus and other tyrannosaurids were probably attracted by the smell of blood and may have fought over a kill.

FACTFILE: ALBERTOSAURUS

Lived: 75 to 65 million years ago

Group: Theropoda

Size: 9 m (30 feet) long

Weight: 2-3 tonnes

Discovery: 1892, Alberta, Canada

Diet: carnivore

Special features: powerful legs, tiny arms

Name means: 'Alberta reptile'

PREDATORS

The first theropods had long arms and strong hands, with five fingers. They may have used the fingers to seize and hold down their prey. Dinosaurs that came later, such as *Tyrannosaurus*, had short arms with two fingers, and short, strong thigh bones. This means that these later theropods may have been good runners. Theropods had bladelike, jagged teeth that curved into the mouth. Once the theropod sunk its jaws into its victim's flesh, the prey could not escape.

Theropods may have hunted in packs. Big predators, such as *Tyrannosaurus* and *Allosaurus,* probably hunted alone. They chased their prey, wrestled it to the ground, and killed it by biting its neck. This is how lions and tigers hunt today. Large theropods probably hunted by stealth – staying very still until a plant-eater came near, or creeping slowly through the trees and bushes, until they were within striking distance. Then, with a quick leap, they would capture their prey!

Run for your life!
T. rex *had massive jaws and a powerful neck. This suggests that the dinosaur hunted by charging at its prey, such as this duckbill, and hitting it hard. Then T. rex would snap its huge jaws shut around the animal's neck.*

THE THEROPODS:

- *Albertosaurus*
- *Allosaurus*
- *Avimimus*
- *Ceratosaurus*
- *Coelophysis*
- *Compsognathus*
- *Daspletosaurus*

- *Deinonychus*
- *Dilophosaurus*
- *Dromaeosaurus*
- *Dromiceiomimus*
- *Ornitholestes*
- *Oviraptor*
- *Saurornithoides*

- *Segisaurus*
- *Struthiomimus*
- *Troodon*
- *Tyrannosaurus*
- *Velociraptor*

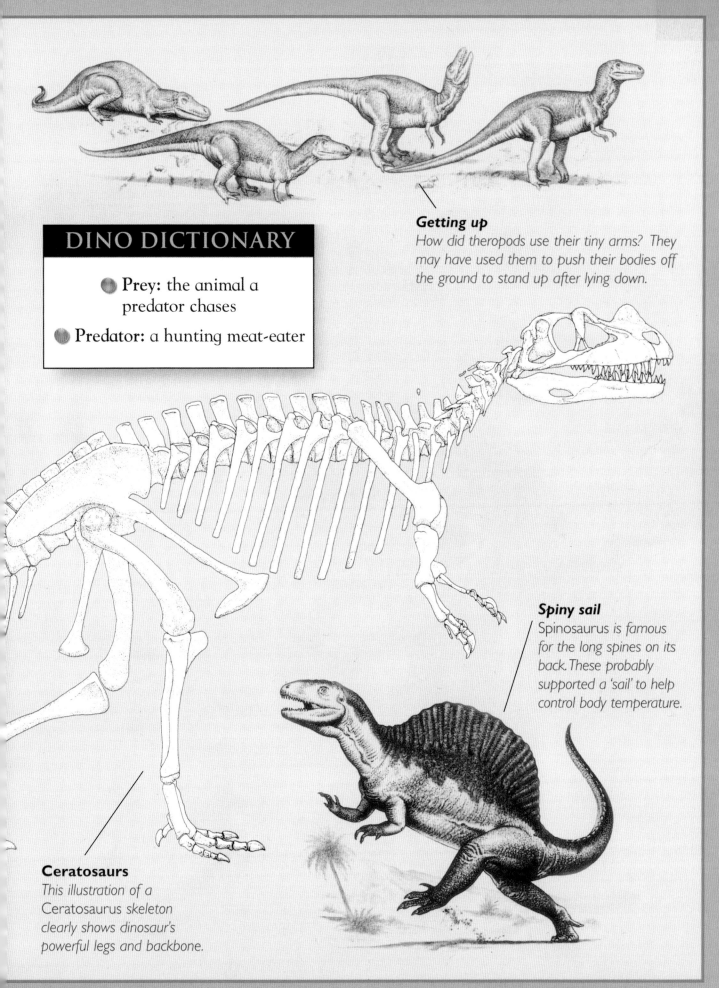

DINO DICTIONARY

- **Prey:** the animal a predator chases
- **Predator:** a hunting meat-eater

Getting up

How did theropods use their tiny arms? They may have used them to push their bodies off the ground to stand up after lying down.

Spiny sail

Spinosaurus is famous for the long spines on its back. These probably supported a 'sail' to help control body temperature.

Ceratosaurs

This illustration of a Ceratosaurus skeleton clearly shows dinosaur's powerful legs and backbone.

TWO-LEGGED RUNNERS

Whether they were as small as turkeys or as big as elephants, the two-footed plant-eating ornithopods all had one thing in common – their bird-like feet.

UNUSUAL DEFENCES

The main group of small, plant-eating dinosaurs were the ornithopods. Some had unusual armour and eating habits.

The first ornithopods lived during the late Triassic Period. They were small, fast-moving, two-legged animals. The earliest ornithopod was *Lesothosaurus*, which was about the size of a cat. It could dart quickly to escape predators. Its head was primitive and lizardlike compared to later ornithopods. Its larger relative, *Scutellosaurus*, had rows of armour plates along its body. These were set into the skin like the bony scales of a crocodile.

   Heterodontosaurus was similar to *Lesothosaurus*, but it had larger feet and various-sized teeth. It fed differently from *Lesothosaurus*. Instead of just swallowing food, *Heterodontosaurus* chewed everything in its cheek. The long fangs at the sides of the dinosaur's mouth may have been used to dig up roots from the ground.

HOW DO I SAY THAT?

● **HETERODONTOSAURUS**
HET-ER-OH-DON'T-OH-SAW-RUS
● **LESOTHOSAURUS**
LESS-OH-TOE-SAW-RUS
● **SCUTELLOSAURUS**
SCOOT-ELL-OH-SAW-RUS

Lesothosaurus
This dinosaur was one of the smallest plant-eaters. It used its small, powerful arms to gather up leaves and other plant food to stuff into its mouth. It had lots of sharp, evenly spaced teeth and slender jaws.

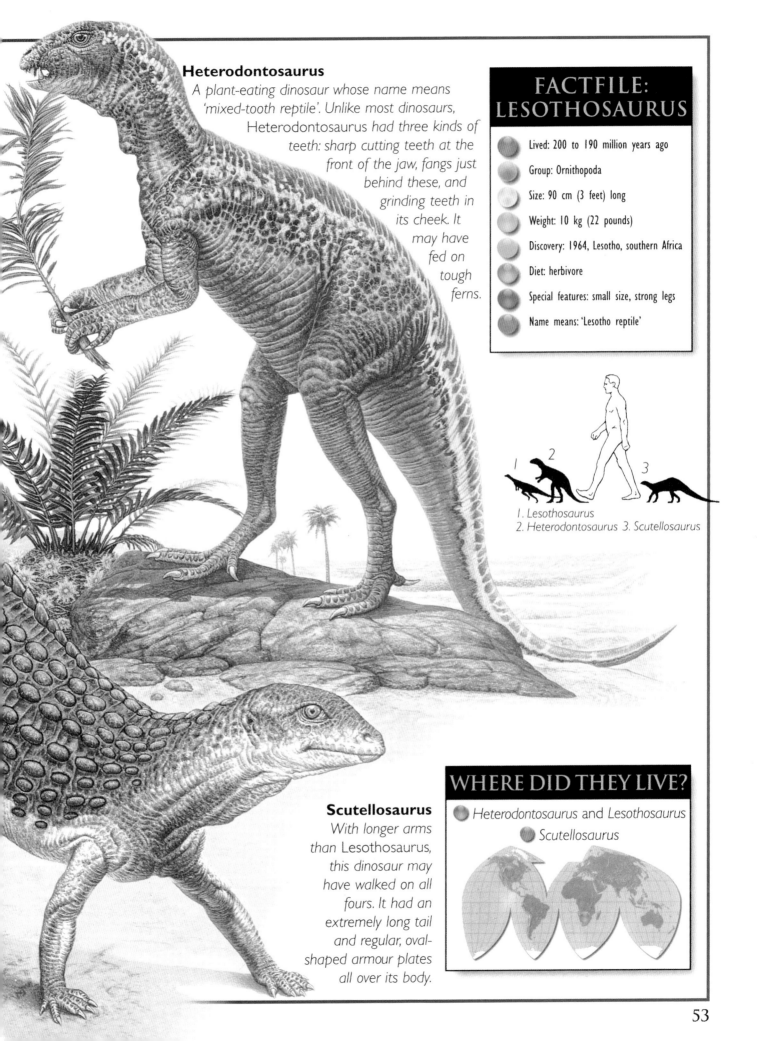

Heterodontosaurus

A plant-eating dinosaur whose name means 'mixed-tooth reptile'. Unlike most dinosaurs, Heterodontosaurus had three kinds of teeth: sharp cutting teeth at the front of the jaw, fangs just behind these, and grinding teeth in its cheek. It may have fed on tough ferns.

FACTFILE: LESOTHOSAURUS

- Lived: 200 to 190 million years ago
- Group: Ornithopoda
- Size: 90 cm (3 feet) long
- Weight: 10 kg (22 pounds)
- Discovery: 1964, Lesotho, southern Africa
- Diet: herbivore
- Special features: small size, strong legs
- Name means: 'Lesotho reptile'

1. Lesothosaurus
2. Heterodontosaurus 3. Scutellosaurus

Scutellosaurus

With longer arms than Lesothosaurus, this dinosaur may have walked on all fours. It had an extremely long tail and regular, oval-shaped armour plates all over its body.

WHERE DID THEY LIVE?

Heterodontosaurus and Lesothosaurus

Scutellosaurus

53

SPEEDY & BIRD-LIKE

It was once thought that primitive ornithopods lived in trees, grasping branches with their feet like giant birds.

The best-known primitive ornithopod is *Hypsilophodon*. When the first fossils of *Hypsilophodon* were found in 1849, scientists thought that they were the bones of a young *Iguanodon*. After more fossils were found, scientists realized this was a completely new dinosaur. Similar fossils have been found all over the world. The biggest *Hypsilophodon* relative was *Tenontosaurus* from North America.

   Hypsilophodon and its relatives were small and agile dinosaurs, with long, slender four-toed back legs. They had short front legs and stubby five-fingered hands. Their long fingers and toes led scientists to think that they might have been good at climbing trees. However, the muscles in their legs indicate that they were probably fast land runners. *Hypsilophodon* and its relatives had powerful jaws and grinding teeth. This helped them to chew tough plant material efficiently.

Hypsilophodon
This dinosaur had strong back legs and a horny beak for snipping off leaves. Hypsilodophodon had four fingers and a little spike on each hand.

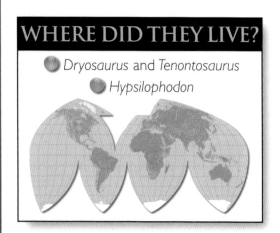

WHERE DID THEY LIVE?
● *Dryosaurus* and *Tenontosaurus*
● *Hypsilophodon*

1. *Dryosaurus* 2. *Hypsilophodon* 3. *Tenontosaurus*

Tenontosaurus

A much bigger dinosaur than other Hypsilophodon, Tenontosaurus weighed around one tonne. It had a powerful tail, which might have been used to strike attacking predators, such as Deinonychus.

FACTFILE: HYPSILOPHODON

- Lived: 140 to 120 million years ago
- Group: Ornithopoda
- Size: 2 m (6 1/2 feet) long
- Weight: 50 kg (110 pounds)
- Discovery: 1849, England, U.K.
- Diet: herbivore
- Special features: strong legs, beak
- Name means: 'high-ridged tooth'

Dryosaurus

Like Hypsilophodon, Dryosaurus had a horny beak, but it had no front teeth. With its powerful back legs, this dinosaur was able to wander great distances, and the species spread all over the world.

HOW DO I SAY THAT?

DRYOSAURUS
DRY-OH-SAW-RUS

HYPSILOPHODON
HIP-SIL-OAF-OH-DON

TENONTOSAURUS
TEN-ONT-OH-SAW-RUS

FAST RUNNERS

Hypsilophodon was one of the most successful small ornithopods. *Hypsilophodon* was similar to iguanodontids such as *Iguanodon*. However, *Hypsilophodon* had smaller, more sharply pointed teeth and a horny beak. It also had few teeth at the front of the jaws, and some relatives had even no teeth at all. Many of today's plant-eating animals do not have teeth at the front of their mouths. Sheep, for example, snip off grass by pressing their tongue against a bony plate in the roof of their mouths.

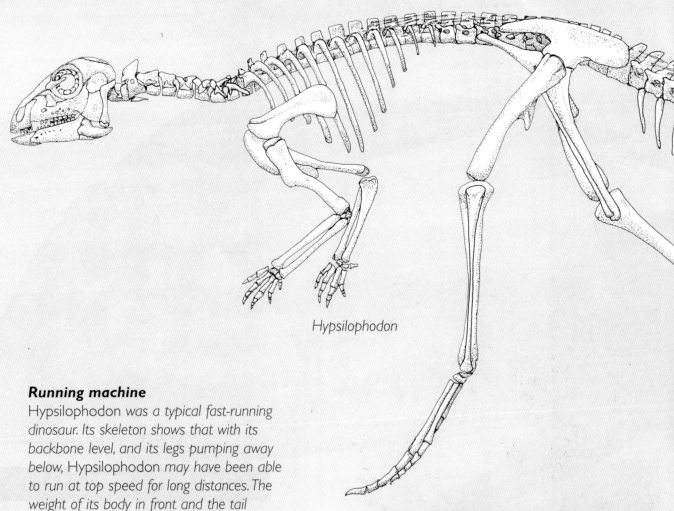

Hypsilophodon

Running machine

Hypsilophodon *was a typical fast-running dinosaur. Its skeleton shows that with its backbone level, and its legs pumping away below,* Hypsilophodon *may have been able to run at top speed for long distances. The weight of its body in front and the tail behind were equal, so* Hypsilophodon *balanced like a seesaw over its back legs.*

DINO DICTIONARY

- **Femur:** the thigh bone
- **Carnivore:** a meat-eating animal

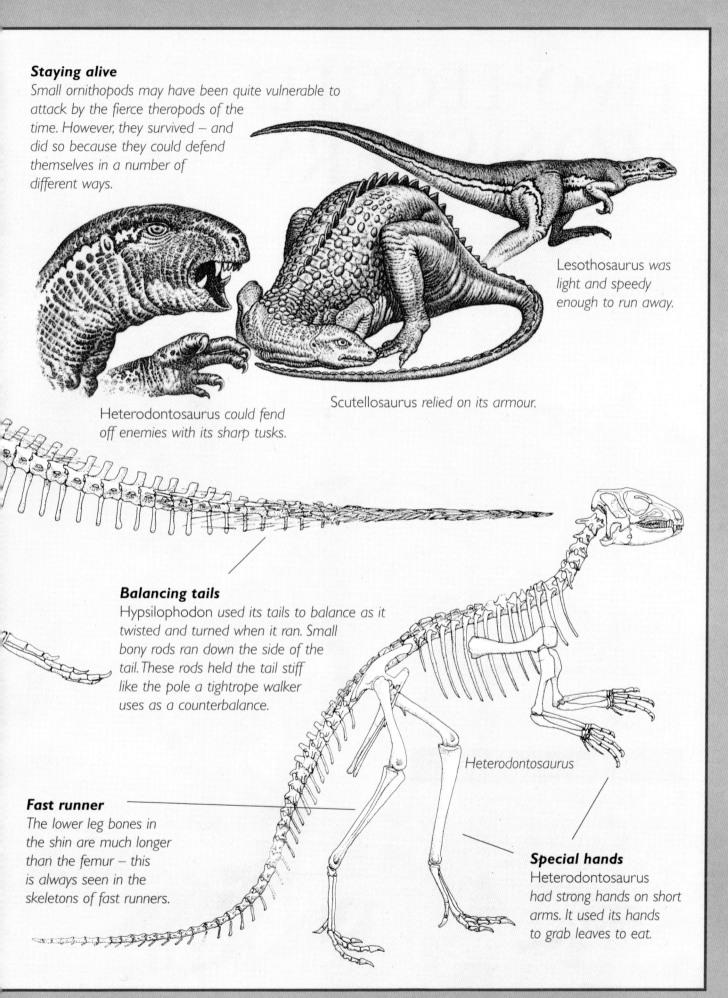

Staying alive

Small ornithopods may have been quite vulnerable to attack by the fierce theropods of the time. However, they survived – and did so because they could defend themselves in a number of different ways.

Lesothosaurus was light and speedy enough to run away.

Heterodontosaurus could fend off enemies with its sharp tusks.

Scutellosaurus relied on its armour.

Balancing tails

Hypsilophodon used its tails to balance as it twisted and turned when it ran. Small bony rods ran down the side of the tail. These rods held the tail stiff like the pole a tightrope walker uses as a counterbalance.

Fast runner

The lower leg bones in the shin are much longer than the femur – this is always seen in the skeletons of fast runners.

Heterodontosaurus

Special hands

Heterodontosaurus had strong hands on short arms. It used its hands to grab leaves to eat.

TWO-LEGGED MONSTERS

These bird-footed runners attacked enemies with a vicious, daggerlike thumb claw.

The best-known ornithopod is *Iguanodon*. Its skeleton was one of the first ever to be found. *Iguanodon* stood and ran on its hind legs, but it could swing down onto its hands to feed on low-lying plants. *Iguanodon* had hooves on its feet, and a mixture of hooves and claws on its hands.

The four ornithopods, shown together in this picture, lived in different parts of the world. *Iguanodon* is best known from fossil finds in Europe. *Ouranosaurus* lived in Africa and *Muttaburrasaurus* in Australia. *Camptosaurus*, an early ornithopod, came from North America.

Camptosaurus
An early ornithopod of the late Jurassic Period.

1. Camptosaurus
2. Ouranosaurus
3. Muttaburrasaurus
4. Iguanodon

HOW DO I SAY THAT?

- **CAMPTOSAURUS**
  KAMP-TOE-SAW-RUS
- **IGUANODON**
  IG-WAN-OH-DON
- **MUTTABURRASAURUS**
  MUT-AH-BUR-AH-SAW-RUS
- **OURANOSAURUS**
  OO-RAN-OH-SAW-RUS

Ouranosaurus
This dinosaur had a sail running along its back and tail.

Muttaburrasaurus
An ornithopod had a bump on its snout.

Defending claw
The large thumb claw of the ornithopods is a mystery. Why would a peaceful plant-eater have had such a lethal weapon? It may have been used to scare enemies away or to attract a mate.

WHERE DID THEY LIVE?

Camptosaurus   Iguanodon
Muttaburrasaurus   Ouranosaurus

Iguanodon
A dinosaur which had huge, three-toed feet. Each toe ended with a small hoof instead of a claw.

HORNBLOWERS

Some hadrosaurs, or duckbilled dinosaurs, were unusual because they had fantastic crests on their heads.

Scientists have debated for years why hadrosaurs had crests on their heads. Some thought they were used for fighting, but because they were hollow, they would probably have been too weak for this purpose. Others thought the crests could have been used as underwater snorkels. This, too, is unlikely because the crests have no opening for breathing. Most scientists now think that the crests were used for signalling and calling to other dinosaurs in the herd.

Each species of hadrosaur had a unique crest shape that made its own sound. Male sounds were different from female sounds. Scientists have made models of the tubes inside the crests to find out what the dinosaurs sounded like. The tubes ran up from the nostrils and down to the throat. When a hadrosaur breathed, the air passed through the crest and made a honking noise.

Tsintaosaurus
The short, tubular crest that pointed forward on the forehead was unusual. Most crests pointed backward.

HOW DO I SAY THAT?

- **CORYTHOSAURUS**
  KOR-ITH-OH-SAW-US
- **PARASAUROLOPHUS**
  PAR-AH-SAWR-OR-LOAF-US
- **SAUROLOPHUS**
  SAWR-OH-LOAF-US
- **TSINTAOSAURUS**
  CHING-DOW-SAW-RUS

Saurolophus
A crestless dinosaur with a strange point at the back of its head. The nasal passages opened into a broad area on top of the snout, which was probably covered with loose skin. Saurolophus could blow up the skin like a balloon and let out a great bellow.

1. Tsintaosaurus 2. Saurolophus 3. Corythosaurus 4. Parasaurolophus

WHERE DID THEY LIVE?

- Corythosaurus and Parasaurolophus
- Saurolophus
- Tsintaosaurus

Parasaurolophus

In addition to a long tube at the back of its head, Parasaurolophus may have had a sail of skin between the crest and the neck. This sail could have been brightly coloured and acted as a signalling device.

Corythosaurus

This dinosaur had a crest shaped like half a dinner plate. Breathing tubes ran around inside the crest like the tubes of a French horn.

FACTFILE: CORYTHOSAURUS

- Lived: 90 to 70 million years ago
- Group: Ornithopoda
- Size: 10 m (33 feet) long
- Weight: 5 tonnes
- Discovery: 1914, Alberta, Canada
- Diet: herbivore
- Special features: platelike head crest
- Name means: 'Corinthian helmet reptile'

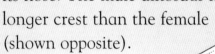

CREST-HEADED HADROSAURS

Crest size and shape may have varied with the dinosaur's age, and whether it was male or female. *Parasaurolophus* had a crest that was more than double the size of its skull. The crest was hollow, with air tubes inside. When *Parasaurolophus* breathed out, it probably made a loud honking noise through its nose. The male dinosaur had a longer crest than the female (shown opposite).

Fast runner
Parasaurolophus *had a powerfully built skeleton. The dinosaur's body was designed for running fast over short distances to escape from predators. The hands bear small hooves on some fingers, and claws on the others. This shows that they were used for both walking and grasping.*

Crestless hadrosaurs

Some scientists believe that the crestless dinosaurs may have had inflatable skin flaps that stretched over their broad snouts.

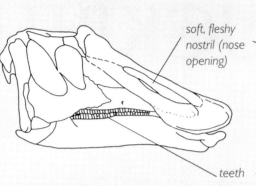

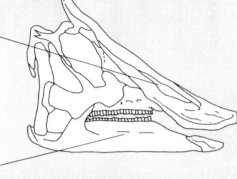

soft, fleshy nostril (nose opening)

teeth

Prosaurolophus *skull*

Sauralophus *skull*

Strong back

Hadrosaurs had a mesh of bony rods along their backbones, which gave them extra strength.

DINO DICTIONARY

- **Skeleton:** the bony framework that supports the body
- **Skull:** the bones of the head

Female head

This cross-section shows the tubes inside the bony crest of a female Parasaurolophus. When the animal breathed, air passed through the nostrils, up one side of the crest, down the other, and then into the throat. There was no hole at the top of the crest, so it could not have been used as a snorkel as scientists once believed. Other hadrosaurs had similar systems of breathing tubes inside their crests.

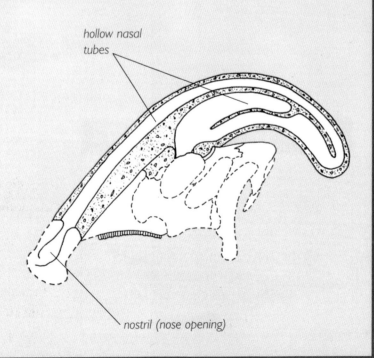

hollow nasal tubes

nostril (nose opening)

THE DUCKBILLS

Recognized by their unusual heads, these fast-running, plant-eating ornithopods appeared late in the dinosaur age.

Hadrosaurs are also called 'duckbills' because of their duck-shaped heads. Duckbills were so similar that their skeletons are almost impossible to tell apart. The main differences are in the shape of the head. *Anatotitan* had a long, low snout. *Bactrosaurus* had a short snout. *Kritosaurus* had a low hump in front of the eyes.

Duckbills lived mainly in North America and Asia, in huge herds made up of different species. They relied on speed to escape from predators. Although they would go on all fours to feed, they rose up on their powerful back legs to run. Their tails stuck out behind as a counterbalance.

Out of water
Scientists used to think that duckbills, like Kritosaurus, lived in water. Their flattened tails and hands looked good for swimming. However, now they are believed to have been forest-living animals.

HOW DO I SAY THAT?

⬤ ANATOTITAN
AH-NAT-OH-TEE-TAN

⬤ BACTROSAURUS
BAK-TRO-SAW-RUS

⬤ EDMONTOSAURUS
ED-MONT-OH-SAW-RUS

⬤ KRITOSAURUS
KRIT-OH-SAW-RUS

FACTFILE: EDMONTOSAURUS

- Lived: 75 to 65 million years ago
- Group: Ornithopoda
- Size: 10-13 m (33-43 feet) long
- Weight: 8-10 tonnes
- Discovery: 1892, Alberta, Canada
- Diet: herbivore
- Special features: duck-like snout, hooves on hand
- Name means: 'Edmonton reptile'

1. Bactrosaurus   2. Kritosaurus   3. Anatotitan   4. Edmontosaurus

Anatotitan and Edmontosaurus

Bactrosaurus   Kritosaurus

Bactrosaurus

This is one of the earliest hadrosaurs. It lived in Asia, so it would not have come across the three other North American dinosaurs.

Easy eating

Anatotitan shows its 'duckbill', which was used to gather plant food.

Edmontosaurus

One of the largest hadrosaurs, Edmontosaurus had hooved hands and feet, so that it could run on two or four legs.

DUCKBILL HADROSAURS

Ornithopods had a mouthful of blunt teeth, which were perfect for grinding up plants. In fact, the duckbills had up to 300 teeth in each jaw, arranged in several rows. As the top row wore out, the next row moved up to fill the gap.

Duckbills had large nostrils (the big openings at the front of the snout). This means that duckbills may have had a good sense of smell. They also may have been able to snort and bellow through their noses. The nose could have been used for signalling purposes, allowing the duckbill to produce distinctive calls. Some duckbills had such long noses that they could have been used for feeding underwater. The nose could act as a snorkel, so that the creature could breathe while it was eating.

Hooves
Duckbills had small hooves on most fingers, because these dinosaurs walked on all fours.

THE ORNITHOPODS:

- Anatotitan
- Bactrosaurus
- Camptosaurus
- Corythosaurus
- Dryosaurus
- Edmontosaurus
- Heterodontosaurus
- Hypsilophodon
- Iguanodon
- Kritosaurus
- Lesothosaurus
- Maiasaura
- Muttaburrasaurus
- Ouranosaurus
- Parasaurolophus
- Saurolophus
- Scutellosaurus
- Tenontosaurus
- Tsintaosaurus

Bellowing snouts
Duckbill hadrosaurs, such as Edmontosaurus, *could bellow by inflating a balloon-like area of skin over their snouts.*

Back

Ornithopods often had little strips of crisscrossed bone along the backbone. These structures started out as flesh, but turned to bone to strengthen the back as the dinosaur grew older.

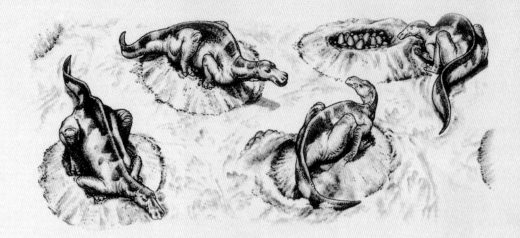

Parental care

Recent discoveries show that dinosaurs cared for their young. Maiasaura, a duckbill hadrosaur, is known as the 'good mother' dinosaur. Like all dinosaurs, it laid its eggs in shallow nests scooped out of the earth. Whole colonies of Maiasaura nests have been found, and there is evidence that the mothers laid their eggs, covered them, and then guarded the nests. It is believed that each female dinosaur in the colony would take care of her eggs, keeping her distance from her neighbours. When the eggs hatched, the parents probably brought them soft plants to eat. This parental care would have continued until the young grew old enough to look after themselves.

Tail

Long, rib-like bones ran underneath the tail. These indicate that the ornithopods had powerful muscles in their tails.

Legs

Ornithopods had strong, pillar-like legs, which were designed for support and long spells of running. They needed these powerful legs so that they could outrun their predators.

DINO DICTIONARY

● **Parental care:** the mother and father look after the young

ARMOURED PLANT-EATERS

Many plant-eating dinosaurs had armour to protect them from the theropods. Stegosaurs had plates, ankylosaurs had chain-mail armour, ceratopsians had horns and pachycephalosaurs had battering rams.

PLATED BEASTS

With its spiky tail and double row of plates running down its back, *Stegosaurus* is one of the best-known dinosaurs.

The huge bony plates that ran down the backs of these dinosaurs may not have been used for defence, since they did not offer much protection. Some scientists think that the plates may have been used to control body temperature. Fossil evidence suggests that the plates may have been covered with skin and a network of blood vessels. On a cool morning, *Stegosaurus* may have stood sideways, with its plates facing the sun, and absorbed heat through the skin and blood vessels. If the dinosaur became too hot, it would then turn away from the sun to cool down.

The tail spikes were almost certainly used as weapons against attack. By swinging its tail, *Stegosaurus* could give its main enemy, *Allosaurus*, a dangerous blow that could rip the predator's belly open.

Tuojiangosaurus
Around 6 m (20 feet) long, this dinosaur was smaller than Stegosaurus. It had smaller plates that were spaced like a fence along its back. The tail spikes were similar in shape to those of Stegosaurus.

Kentrosaurus
This was a small stegosaur – only 2.5 metres (8 feet) long. It had narrow plates and spikes down its back. These may have also covered its hips and shoulders, which may have provided extra defence.

Small head
This view of Stegosaurus shows how tiny the dinosaur's head was compared to its broad back and plates.

FACTFILE: STEGOSAURUS

Lived: 155 to 145 million years ago

Group: Stegosauria

Size: 6-7.5 m (20-25 feet) long

Weight: 5 tonnes

Discovery: 1877, Wyoming, U.S.A.

Diet: herbivore

Special features: plates on back, small head

Name means: 'roofed reptile'

1. Stegosaurus 2. Tuojiangosaurus 3. Kentrosaurus

Stegosaurus
Since they were not fixed to the skeleton, it is hard to know exactly how the plates appeared on the body of Stegosaurus. It is likely that the plates were arranged in a double row on the back, with a slight overlap between each plate.

WHERE DID THEY LIVE?

Kentrosaurus
Stegosaurus   Tuojiangosaurus

HOW DO I SAY THAT?

KENTROSAURUS
KEN-TRO-SAW-RUS

STEGOSAURUS
STEG-OH-SAW-RUS

TUOJIANGOSAURUS
TOO-OH-JEE-ANG-OH-SAW-RUS

71

SPIKES AND PLATES

Stegosaurs had huge arms and legs to support their weight. The broad backbone and ribs carried the heavy back plates and spines. This meant that a stegosaur was not built for speed. The arms were half the length of the legs, making it hard for the stegosaur to run without tipping over on its nose. The dinosaur's head also seems very small compared to the rest of its bulky body.

Dinosaurs had relatively small brains for animals of their size. This is why most scientists think they were not very intelligent. *Stegosaurus* is considered to have been a less intelligent dinosaur. For an animal that weighed more than the largest living elephant, *Stegosaurus* had a tiny brain – about the size of a walnut. If you compare this to mammals today, the brain of *Stegosaurus* was the right size for a kitten!

Plates
The patterns of ridges and channels show where the skin and blood vessels lay over the plates.

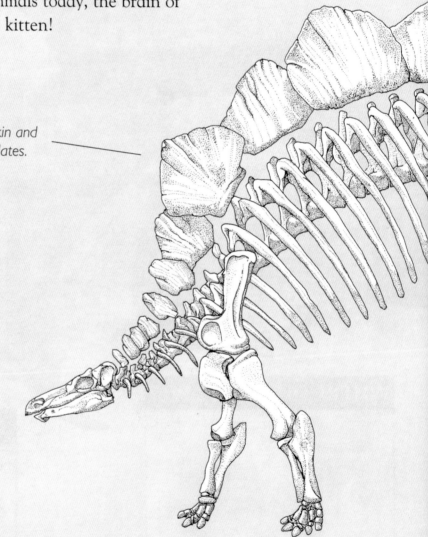

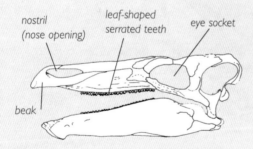

nostril
(nose opening)

leaf-shaped
serrated teeth

eye socket

beak

Head
The narrow skull of Stegosaurus had a tiny space for the brain at the back. The front of the mouth did not contain teeth, and was probably covered with a horny beak for snipping off plants. The small back teeth were used to chop up soft plants.

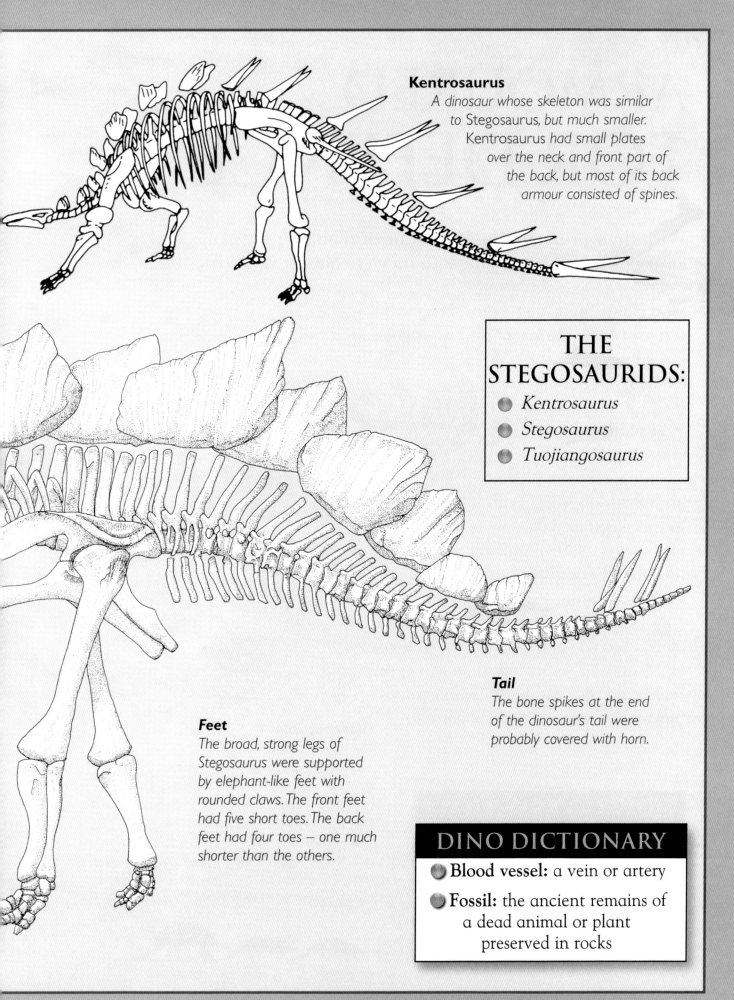

Kentrosaurus

A dinosaur whose skeleton was similar to Stegosaurus, but much smaller. Kentrosaurus had small plates over the neck and front part of the back, but most of its back armour consisted of spines.

THE STEGOSAURIDS:

- *Kentrosaurus*
- *Stegosaurus*
- *Tuojiangosaurus*

Tail
The bone spikes at the end of the dinosaur's tail were probably covered with horn.

Feet
The broad, strong legs of Stegosaurus were supported by elephant-like feet with rounded claws. The front feet had five short toes. The back feet had four toes – one much shorter than the others.

DINO DICTIONARY

- **Blood vessel:** a vein or artery
- **Fossil:** the ancient remains of a dead animal or plant preserved in rocks

ARMOURED FOR DEFENCE

With their protective body armour of regular bony plates and larger pieces of bone, ankylosaurs were almost indestructible.

Most plant-eating, four-footed, armoured dinosaurs, such as *Hylaeosaurus* and *Nodosaurus,* lived toward the end of the dinosaur age during the Cretaceous Period. They needed to be armed for defence against meat-eating predators, and relied on a rugged chain mail of bony plates. Nodosaurid ankylosaurs had narrow heads, pointed tails and leathery skin that was studded with bony lumps. Some had rows of long spikes along each side of the body. They were stocky, heavy animals, with short, stout legs to support their great body weight. If *Tyrannosaurus rex* had tried to attack these dinosaurs, it would have broken its teeth.

Hylaeosaurus
The third dinosaur ever discovered was named Hylaeosaurus in 1833. Only the front part of this creature is known from fossil evidence. Protective armour is obvious — the neck and body were covered by rings of tough chain mail, made up of small bony plates that locked together. Larger bone knobs ran in rows down the middle of the dinosaur's back, and rows of long, sturdy spikes ran along each side of its body.

HOW DO I SAY THAT?

- **HYLAEOSAURUS**
  HIGH-LEE-OH-SAW-RUS
- **NODOSAURUS**
  NODE-OH-SAW-RUS
- **POLACANTHUS**
  POLE-AH-KAN-THUS

1. Hylaeosaurus 2. Polacanthus 3. Nodosaurus

Nodosaurus

This large dinosaur did not have spikes, but its well-organized body armour was just as tough. Even fearsome T. rex would not have been strong enough to break through the tightly locked, square-shaped plates that covered its back. Nodosaurus came from North America and would not have lived with the other dinosaurs shown here.

FACTFILE: HYLAEOSAURUS

- Lived: 130 to 115 million years ago
- Group: Ankylosauria
- Size: 4 m (13 feet) long
- Weight: 1 tonne
- Discovery: 1833, England, U.K.
- Diet: herbivore
- Special features: bony armour, spikes
- Name means: 'woodland reptile'

WHERE DID THEY LIVE?

- *Hylaeosaurus* and *Polacanthus*
- *Nodosaurus*

Polacanthus

Like Hylaeosaurus, *fossil skeletons of* Polacanthus *are incomplete. The tough armour plates and spines can survive in rocks where softer bones have been lost.*

CLUB-TAILED DINOSAURS

Some ankylosaurs not only had full body armour but also giant bony clubs at the ends of their tails.

Measuring some 6 metres (20 feet) long, and weighing more than 3 tonnes, ankylosaurs, such as *Euoplocephalus*, were like huge tanks. When these imposing creatures were attacked, they would crouch down toward the ground and rely on their invincible armour to protect themselves from predators. Their clubbed tails were strong and could make accurate blows when defence was required.

Since they were herbivores (plant-eaters), ankylosaurs had small, leaf-shaped teeth and horny beaks. Mostly, they swallowed their food whole. Plant food is difficult to digest, which is why ankylosaurs had barrel-like bodies and enormous stomachs. Imagine the rumblings and explosions after an ankylosaur had eaten its lunch!

Euoplocephalus
This dinosaur had an extra layer of bony plates on top of the skull bones. The four spines around the back of the head provided extra protection. Even the eyelids had a bony cover.

1. *Pinacosaurus* 2. *Euoplocephalus*

HOW DO I SAY THAT?

● EUOPLOCEPHALUS
YOO-OP-LO-KEF-AL-US

● PINACOSAURUS
PIN-AK-OH-SAW-RUS

FACTFILE: EUOPLOCEPHALUS

- Lived: 80 to 70 million years ago
- Group: Ankylosauria
- Size: 6 m (20 feet) long
- Weight: 2-3 tonnes
- Discovery: 1902, Alberta, Canada
- Diet: herbivore
- Special features: armour spikes, tail club
- Name means: 'true-plated head'

Pinacosaurus

A dinosaur which had an armoured, knobbly skull, and dense armour plates over its neck, back and tail. The dinosaur's tail club was huge. It was made of bone that was fixed to the backbone at the end of the tail. This was a fearsome weapon that could have knocked any predator senseless.

WHERE DID THEY LIVE?

Euoplocephalus   Pinacosaurus

UP CLOSE

ARMED DINOSAURS

An ankylosaur skeleton was designed to support the huge weight of the armour. The bony plates and spines provided great protection, so these dinosaurs did not need to run fast to escape from predators. Ankylosaur arms and legs were short and pillar-like, just like those of an elephant today. The ribs and backbone were strong to carry the armour and the large stomach. The small head was protected by rock-hard armour. The tail had strong muscles that ran down each side, and the ankylosaur could swing its tail club with enough force to kill a predator.

Rock solid

When it was attacked, Hylaeosaurus probably defended itself by crouching down, tucking its arms and legs under its body, and waiting for the predator to go away. The armour plates and the spikes on the sides of the body prevented the predator from reaching any fleshy part of the body.

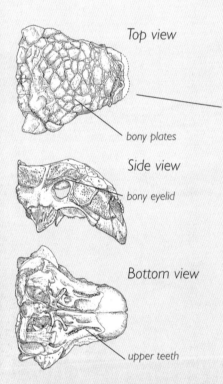

Top view

bony plates

Side view

bony eyelid

Bottom view

upper teeth

Skull

Different views of an ankylosaur skull show the extra layers of thick, bony armour. A mosaic of small bones covered the normal skull bones. Each ankylosaur species had a different pattern of skull armour. The bony eyelid and the tiny teeth can also be seen in the side view and bottom view.

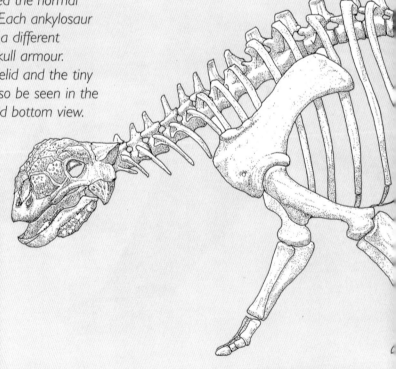

DINO DICTIONARY

● **Girdle:** a bony arch to which an arm or leg is attached

● **Vertebra:** one of the bones that make up the backbone

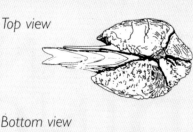

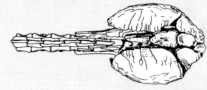
Bottom view

Side view

Powerful weapon

The ankylosaurids protected themselves by giving meat-eating dinosaurs a mighty slap with their massive tail clubs. A well-aimed blow could easily have killed a predatory dinosaur such as T. rex.

Tail clubs

The tail end of Ankylosaurus was made up from two bony knobs, or plates, that formed in the skin. These were fused to both sides of the vertebrae in the tail.

Euoplocephalus skeleton

The strong shoulder and hip girdles were designed to stand up to huge forces. The hip bones were strengthened, because they were fixed to seven or eight joined vertebrae, forming a wall. This partly supported the weight of the body armour, but it also provided attachments for the tail muscles.

THE ANKYLOSAURS:

- *Ankylosaurus*
- *Euoplocephalus*
- *Hylaeosaurus*
- *Nodosaurus*
- *Pinacosaurus*
- *Polacanthus*

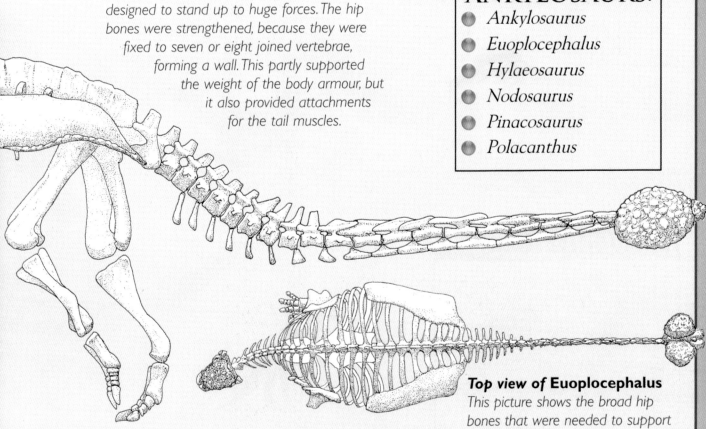

Top view of Euoplocephalus

This picture shows the broad hip bones that were needed to support the heavy armour.

HORNLESS DINOSAURS

Early ceratopsians were small, two-legged dinosaurs that were different from their giant relatives, but they lived in a similar way.

Most of the horn-faced dinosaurs, like *Triceratops* and *Styracosaurus*, were large, four-legged, tank-like animals with huge heads, neck frills, and sharp beaks. But the first ceratopsian, *Psittacosaurus*, was human-sized and stood upright on its back legs. Unlike the later ceratopsians, *Psittacosaurus* had no horns. Neither did it sport a big, bony neck frill. Its long legs and powerful grasping hands were similar to those found in ornithopods, such as *Hypsilophodon*. So what made it a ceratopsian? The clue is in the shape of its mouth – it was curved like a parrot's beak.

Skeleton

Psittacosaurus *was a slender, two-legged dinosaur, like most ornithopods. However, the sturdy front legs may have been used for walking. The hooked beak suggests that* Psittacosaurus *ate tough plant food, maybe even tree branches.*

WHERE DID THEY LIVE?

● Psittacosaurus

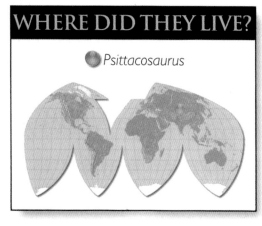

Psittacosaurus

FACTFILE: PSITTACOSAURUS

- Lived: 100 to 90 million years ago
- Group: Ceratopsia
- Size: 1.8 m (6 feet) long
- Weight: 110 pounds (50 kg)
- Discovery: 1922, Mongolia
- Diet: herbivore
- Special features: parrot-like beak, strong hands
- Name means: 'parrot reptile'

Plant-eater

Psittacosaurus *fed on leaves and fruit from trees, which it nipped off with its beak and then crushed and sliced at the back of its mouth.*

Little dinosaurs

Baby Psittacosaurus *skeletons were tiny – about the same size as a pigeon. Young dinosaurs had much weaker jaws than adults, so they probably ate tender shoots and berries.*

HOW DO I SAY THAT?

PSITTACOSAURUS
SIT-AK-OH-SAW-RUS

HORNED GIANTS

Many ceratopsians had horns on the nose and face, as well as a bony shield to protect the neck.

Ceratopsians lived in the late Cretaceous Period. Large numbers of fossil skeletons have been found in the same place, so these dinosaurs probably lived in big herds. Ceratopsians may look fierce, but they were in fact plant-eaters. They had many small teeth that could chop through plant stems and other tough vegetation.

The most famous ceratopsian is *Triceratops*. It had a classic ceratopsian nose horn, which was similar to the horn of a rhinoceros. It also had two larger horns – one over each eye. If *Triceratops* lowered its head and faced its deadly enemy, *Tyrannosaurus rex*, it would have been hard for the predator to attack without getting badly hurt. *Centrosaurus*, a close relative of *Triceratops*, had one huge single horn on its nose and two smaller horns curling over its neck shield, or frill.

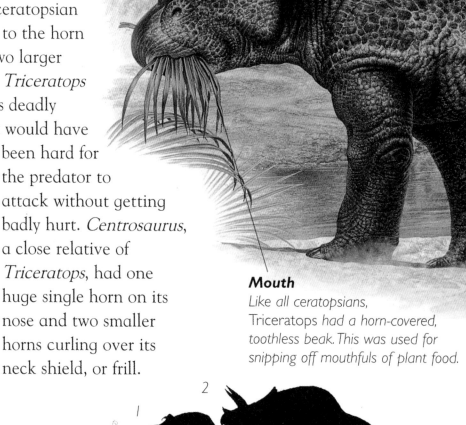

Mouth
Like all ceratopsians, Triceratops had a horn-covered, toothless beak. This was used for snipping off mouthfuls of plant food.

1. Centrosaurus
2. Triceratops

FACTFILE: TRICERATOPS

- Lived: 75 to 65 million years ago
- Group: Ceratopsia
- Size: 9 m (30 feet) long
- Weight: 6 tonnes
- Discovery: 1887, Colorado, U.S.A.
- Diet: herbivore
- Special features: three horns, neck frill
- Name means: 'three-horned face'

HOW DO I SAY THAT?

CENTROSAURUS
SEN-TRO-SAW-RUS

TRICERATOPS
TRY-SER-AH-TOPS

WHERE DID THEY LIVE?

Centrosaurus Triceratops

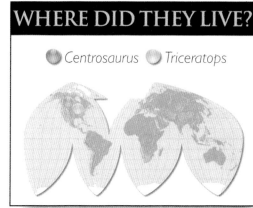

Neck shield

At the back of the head of Triceratops was a long neck shield made of bone and covered with skin. The edge was lined with diamond-shaped bony studs. This giant frill protected the dinosaur's fleshy neck from attack by predators.

Spikes and curls

Centrosaurus had a neck shield made from a broad rim of bone that surrounded two big holes. These holes were probably filled with muscle and covered with skin. The back edge of the neck shield was lined with small spikes. Curling over the top were two sharp horns.

LONG-FRILLED DINOSAURS

Some dinosaurs not only had vicious face horns, but also long heads with huge neck shields, known as frills.

The massive neck frills and horns of ceratopsians must have been heavy to carry around. So why did they have them? It is likely that they were used for defence against *Tyrannosaurus rex* and the other huge predators of the late Cretaceous Period. During fights with each other, male ceratopsians might have used their heads as weapons. Perhaps they locked horns like male deer do today, and wrestled with each other until one gave in. Some scientists believe that the frill was an area of bone that held the jaw muscles. It may be that the frills were bright-coloured and used for signalling to other members of the herd.

1. *Chasmosaurus* 2. *Anchiceratops*
3. *Pentaceratops* 4. *Torosaurus*

WHERE DID THEY LIVE?

Anchiceratops and *Chasmosaurus*
Pentaceratops   *Torosaurus*

Chasmosaurus
A dinosaur with a short nose horn, as well as a horn above each eye. The long neck frill was square and edged with spikes. This front view is what T. rex would have been faced with when it tried to attack!

HOW DO I SAY THAT?

- **ANCHICERATOPS**
  AN-KI-SER-AH-TOPS
- **CHASMOSAURUS**
  KAZ-MO-SAW-RUS
- **PENTACERATOPS**
  PEN-TA-SER-AH-TOPS
- **TOROSAURUS**
  TOR-OH-SAW-RUS

Pentaceratops

Although this dinosaur's name means 'five-horned face', it only had three. The other two are not horns but pointed cheek bones below the eyes. The long, wide frill is edged by small, pointed spikes.

Anchiceratops

This dinosaur had long, pointed horns over its eyes and a large neck frill. Sharp horns lined the top edge of the frill. The dinosaur's horn-covered beak was used for snipping ferns and other tough, low-growing plants.

Torosaurus

This dinosaur's head and neck frill was 3.5 metres (11 1/2 feet) long – about the same size as a small car and half the length of the whole animal.

FACTFILE: TOROSAURUS

- Lived: 75 to 65 million years ago
- Group: Ceratopsia
- Size: 7.6 m (25 feet) long
- Weight: 6 tonnes
- Discovery: 1891, Wyoming, U.S.A.
- Diet: herbivore
- Special features: huge skull, long neck frill
- Name means: 'punctured reptile'

UP CLOSE FRILLS AND HORNS

The ceratopsian skeleton was strong, because these dinosaurs needed powerful arms and legs to support their huge weight. The most unusual features of these dinosaurs are their nose horns and neck frills. Most ceratopsians weighed more than a modern elephant, so they were unable to run very fast. When attacked by a carnivore, the main defence of the ceratopsians would have been to stand their ground and show their horns and neck shield. The ceratopsian's skull presented a tough wall of bone and horn. The neck shield might have been used for signalling to other animals and so could have been brightly coloured and patterned with eyespots like a peacock's tail.

As herbivores, ceratopsians probably lived the way cows do today – cropping and chewing plant food all day. The horn-covered beak snipped off plants, and the tooth-lined jaws ground up the plant material. The food then passed down into a huge stomach that was housed in the rib cage.

THE CERATOPSIA:
- *Anchiceratops*
- *Centrosaurus*
- *Chasmosaurus*
- *Pentaceratops*
- *Psittacosaurus*
- *Torosaurus*
- *Triceratops*

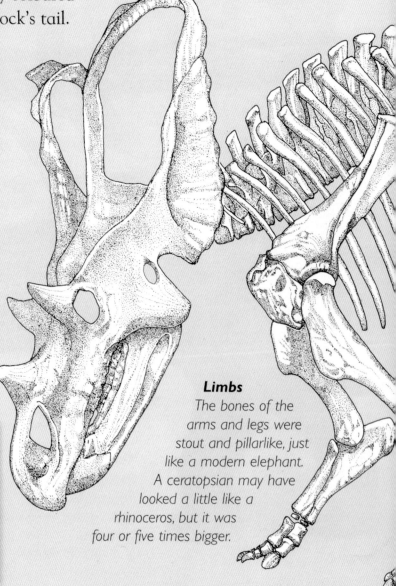

Big head
All ceratopsians had similar skeletons, but each species had a different arrangement of horns and frill. This Chasmosaurus skeleton shows the huge head in relation to the body.

Limbs
The bones of the arms and legs were stout and pillarlike, just like a modern elephant. A ceratopsian may have looked a little like a rhinoceros, but it was four or five times bigger.

DINO DICTIONARY

- **Carnivore:** an animal that feeds on meat
- **Herbivore:** an animal that feeds on plants

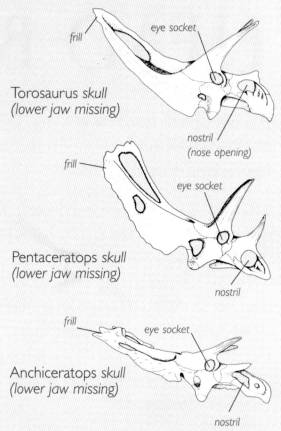

Torosaurus skull
(lower jaw missing)

frill   eye socket

nostril
(nose opening)

Pentaceratops skull
(lower jaw missing)

frill

eye socket

nostril

Anchiceratops skull
(lower jaw missing)

frill   eye socket

nostril

Defence tactics

A herd of ceratopsians may have defended itself from attack by forming a circle around its young. By facing outward with their neck shields lowered and horns pointing straight out, they would have been a tough challenge for predators, such as Tyrannosaurus rex.

Skull shapes

These pictures of ceratopsian skulls show how the lengths of the nose and forehead horns vary between ceratopsians. The bony frill had holes in it to save weight. If the frill had been solid, the dinosaur's head would have been too heavy to lift off the ground!

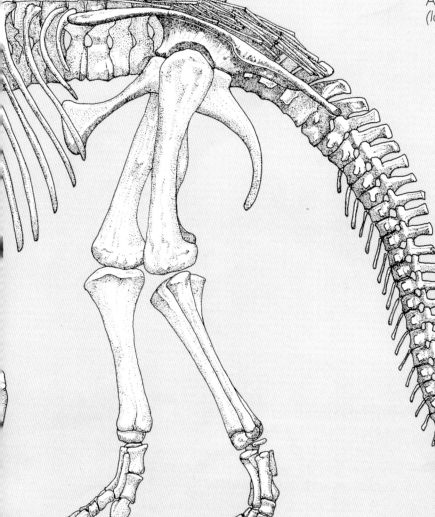

HEAD-BUTTERS

Pachycephalosaurs were an odd group of dinosaurs with their dome-shaped heads and bird-like feet.

The fossilized teeth of a pachycephalosaur were first found in the 1850s, but scientists were unable to figure out what they were. Then, in 1924, a skull and skeleton of *Stegoceras* were discovered. *Stegoceras* was a small, two-legged, plant-eating dinosaur, similar to an ornithopod. But unlike ornithopods, it had a head as strong as a safety helmet. Scientists called this dinosaur a pachycephalosaur.

Why did the pachycephalosaurs have such thick skulls? One of the largest pachycephalosaur was *Pachycephalosaurus*. All its skull bones were of normal thickness for a dinosaur. But the roof bones were 22 cms (8 1/2 inches) thick. The domed head was also rimmed by bony knobs. Pachycephalosaurs may have head-butted each other in fighting rituals, when males tried to win females. The thicker the skull, the more successful the male would be in a contest.

HOW DO I SAY THAT?

● **HOMALOCEPHALE**
HOM-AL-OH-KEF-AL-EE

● **PACHYCEPHALOSAURUS**
PAK-EE-KEF-AL-OH-SAW-RUS

● **STEGOCERAS**
STEG-O-SER-AS

Homalocephale
A 'flat-headed' dinosaur with a lower skull roof than most other pachycephalosaurs.

WHERE DID THEY LIVE?

● Homalocephale
● Pachycephalosaurus ○ Stegoceras

Pachycephalosaurus
The biggest pachycephalosaur was 8 metres (26 feet) long. Only its skull and a few fragments of the skeleton have been found. The thick skulls are more easily preserved as fossils than the other parts of their skeletons. The body of Pachycephalosaurus shown here is based on fossil finds of other, smaller pachycephalosaurs.

1. Stegoceras 2. Homalocephale 3. Pachycephalosaurus

FACTFILE: STEGOCERAS

Lived: 80 to 70 million years ago

Group: Pachycephalosauria

Size: 2 m (6 1/2 feet) long

Weight: 110 pounds (50 kg)

Discovery: 1902, Alberta, Canada

Diet: herbivore

Special features: thick skull roof, bony frill

Name means: 'horny roof'

Stegoceras
*The body shape
of this well-known
pachycephalosaur
is based on several
skeleton finds. Skeletons
of Stegoceras show that
the skull roof grew thicker
as the dinosaur grew older.*

DOME-HEADS

Pachycephalosaurs had light skeletons compared to their thick skulls. The teeth were very small, which means that pachycephalosaurs must have fed on soft plants. Like the ornithopods, pachycephalosaurs had long, slender legs. This would have made them good two-legged runners. It is likely that their main defence from the meat-eaters was speed.

A pachycephalosaur involved in a head-butting contest would have charged forward very quickly – its backbone level and head lowered. As the two animals crashed heads, the force of the blow would have run through the skull and down the neck, producing a loud, cracking sound. This would have shaken the brains of these dinosaurs. But they had such small brains, that it probably did not matter much!

Neck bones
Not much is known about the bones in the neck of Stegoceras. Scientists believe that they must have been especially strong to absorb some of the energy of the impact when skulls crashed together during fights.

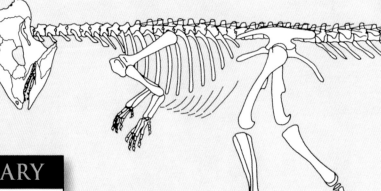

Head
In the head-butting position, the backbone was held straight when the pachycephalosaur ran at the speed of a racehorse. The top of the skull was rounded, so that the impact of the blow would be hardest in the middle. The heads of two head-butters in a contest would face toward the side.

Grasping hands
Stegoceras had five digits on each hand. These would have been useful for grasping and grabbing bunches of leaves.

DINO DICTIONARY

● **Paleontologist:** a person who studies fossils

Skull shapes

Heads of pachycephalosaurs varied
in shape. Some, such as the head of
Pachycephalosaurus, were completely
rounded. Others, such as Homalocephale,
were lower and sloped up to a point at the
back. All the pachycephalosaurs had bony
knobs and hornlets on their snouts and
around the edges of the thickened skull roof.
This edging is like the frill at the back of a
ceratopsian skull. It suggests that these
dinosaur groups were probably close relatives.

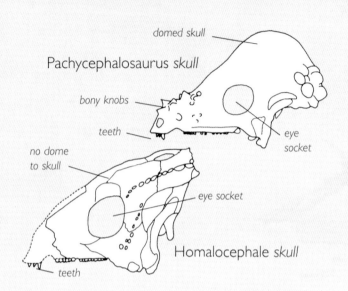

Pachycephalosaurus skull

domed skull

bony knobs

teeth

eye
socket

no dome
to skull

eye socket

Homalocephale skull

teeth

Head-cracking fun

Scientists believe that the clash of heads
sent out loud bangs that would have been
heard from long distances away. Today,
mountain goats and bighorn sheep crash
heads in a similar way during fights.

THE
PACHYCEPHALOSAURIDS:

- *Homalocephale*
- *Pachycephalosaurus*
- *Stegoceras*

Stegoceras

Not much is known about the skeleton of
Stegoceras. Many of the faded elements
shown here have been reconstructed using
the skeletons of other pachycephalosaurs.

MONSTER FLIERS

While dinosaurs roamed the land, leathery-winged reptiles were as common in the skies as birds are today. These flying reptiles were not dinosaurs, but pterosaurs.

FIRST BIRDS?

During the age of the dinosaurs, the skies were ruled by the pterosaurs or 'winged reptiles'. Some were the size of pigeons, but others were monster gliders.

Were pterosaurs ancestors of lizards, birds or bats? Fossil evidence shows that pterosaurs appeared at the beginning of the dinosaur age. Scientists think that they are close relatives of the land-living dinosaurs, because of the shape of their skull and their upright legs. Pterosaurs may have evolved from the flying reptiles of earlier times. These creatures looked like winged lizards. Birds have also been thought of as modern-day pterosaurs. However, birds appeared halfway through the dinosaur age, and are physically similar to the dinosaurs. Like the pterosaurs, birds probably evolved directly from the dinosaurs. Bats appeared after the pterosaurs died out. Yet they have more in common with the prehistoric pterosaurs than birds.

Early fliers
The first pterosaurs appeared during the Triassic Period. They had long wings, prominent wrist bones, pointed teeth, sharp beaks and unusual-shaped heads and jaws.

DINO DICTIONARY

● **Ancestor:** the animal or plant species from which a group arose

● **Evolve:** develop over a long time

Monsters in the sky

The largest pterosaurs appeared in the Cretaceous Period. Many different flyers swirled through the skies during this time. Pterosaurs had diversified into different species, with different-shaped beaks, jaws and head crests to suit their lifestyles.

Jurassic treasures

Most of the information about pterosaurs comes from the huge number of fossils found in the Solnhofen quarries in Southern Germany. In the late Jurassic times, Solnhofen was covered by a lagoon filled with stagnant water. It was flanked by mountains to the north and the deeper waters of what is now the Mediterranean Sea. When flying animals and sea creatures died, they were buried along with the fine sediment that settled at the bottom of the lagoon. The number of perfect fossils found at Solnhofen has made it one of the most treasured sites among fossil scientists.

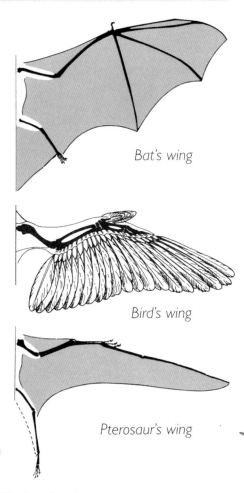

Bat's wing

Bird's wing

Pterosaur's wing

Bird or bat?

A wing has to be a special shape so that an animal can fly. The wings of bats, birds and pterosaurs are similar in shape, but their bone construction is different. This suggests that these animals evolved from different ancestors.

THE WINGED ONES

There were two groups of pterosaurs. The rhamphorhynchoids appeared early in the Triassic Period. The second, more advanced group, the pterodactyloids, followed toward the end of the Jurassic Period.

Pterosaurs probably flew like modern birds. Small ones could flap their wings to lift themselves. Larger pterosaurs may have soared on warm air currents. They relied on the shape of their wings to move through the air like gliders. Unlike birds, pterosaur wings were made of skin that stretched along the arm bone. Fossils of pterosaur wing membranes show that the wings were stiffened by rods of gristle that fanned out from the arms. This pattern of rods is similar to the bony structure that supports the feathers on a bird's wing. Paleontologists disagree on how the wings were attached to the pterosaur's body. The wings may have been attached to the trunk, the legs, or they may have reached down to the knees or even the ankles.

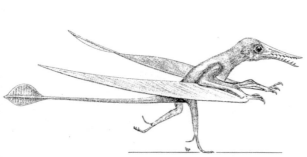

Teeth
The narrow, pointed jaws were lined with different-sized, forward-pointing teeth.

Rhamphorhynchoid features
This group was named after Rhamphorhynchus. It had a slender skeleton, short neck and wrist bones, and a long tail. The long, narrow wings consisted of bones of equal lengths.

On the ground
Did pterosaurs run on their back legs like small bird-footed dinosaurs? Scientists once thought that pterosaurs tucked up their wings under their arms to walk on two legs. Fossil footprints later showed that they actually walked on all fours, using their hands on the their wings as well as their feet.

Long tail
The stiff tail, lined with thin bony rods, may have acted as a rudder – for steering and balancing during flight.

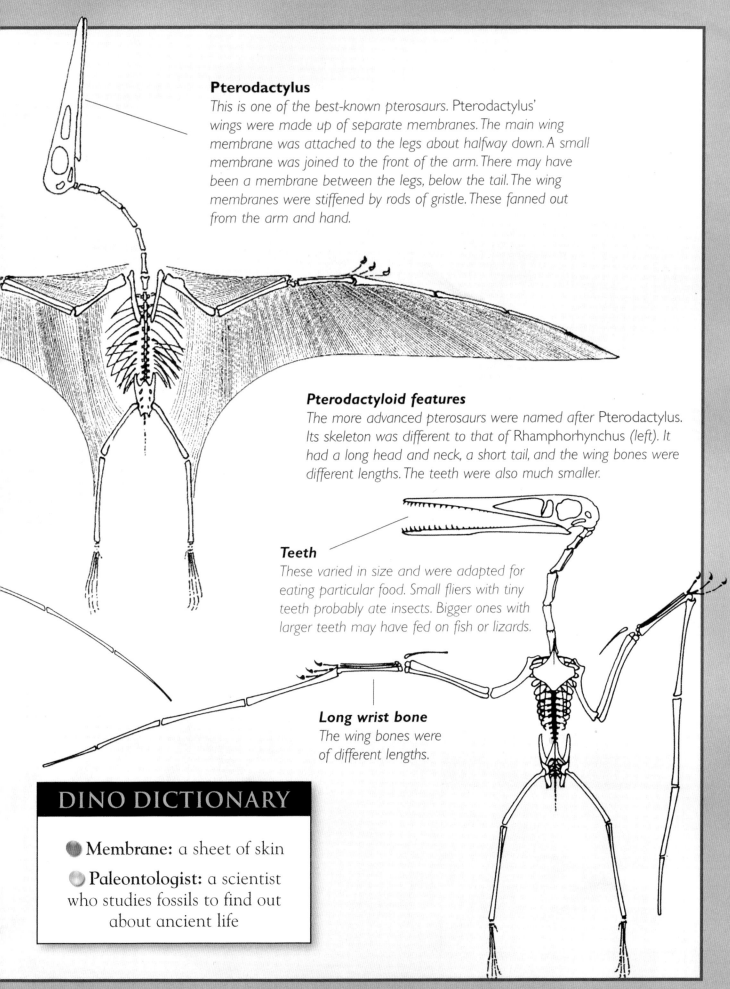

Pterodactylus

This is one of the best-known pterosaurs. Pterodactylus'
wings were made up of separate membranes. The main wing
membrane was attached to the legs about halfway down. A small
membrane was joined to the front of the arm. There may have
been a membrane between the legs, below the tail. The wing
membranes were stiffened by rods of gristle. These fanned out
from the arm and hand.

Pterodactyloid features

The more advanced pterosaurs were named after Pterodactylus.
Its skeleton was different to that of Rhamphorhynchus (left). It
had a long head and neck, a short tail, and the wing bones were
different lengths. The teeth were also much smaller.

Teeth

These varied in size and were adapted for
eating particular food. Small fliers with tiny
teeth probably ate insects. Bigger ones with
larger teeth may have fed on fish or lizards.

Long wrist bone

The wing bones were
of different lengths.

DINO DICTIONARY

● **Membrane:** a sheet of skin

● **Paleontologist:** a scientist
who studies fossils to find out
about ancient life

RISE OF THE PTEROSAURS

Fossils of the earliest pterosaurs show that from the beginning they had all the key features that made them successful fliers.

The earliest pterosaur fossils have been found in rocks in Europe that date from the late Triassic Period. They include *Eudimorphodon* and *Peteinosaurus.* Fossils of these early pterosaurs indicate that they had already evolved the main features of a typical pterosaur. They had large wings that were made from stretchy skin and supported by rods of gristle. Each wing was stretched out by the bones of the arm and hand. The long bones of the fourth finger supported at least half of the wing's length. The first three fingers formed small claws about halfway along the front of the wing. The skeleton of a pterosaur shows that it was probably a strong flier. Pterosaur bones were thin, fragile, and full of holes to make them light. The skull was long and pointed. The shoulder bones and muscles were very strong. This meant that pterosaurs probably flapped their wings to fly. For a long time, however, scientists thought that pterosaurs could only glide through the air.

Eudimorphodon's skeleton

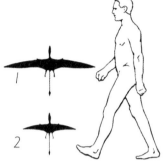

1. *Eudimorphodon*
2. *Peteinosaurus*

Peteinosaurus

This pterosaur had long fangs at the front of its mouth and smaller pointed teeth behind. This indicates that it may have been an insect-eater that fed on large beetles and cockroaches.

WHERE DID THEY LIVE?

Eudimorphodon and *Peteinosaurus*

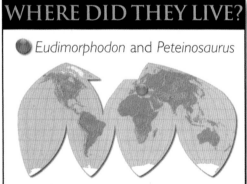

Earliest pterosaur

Eudimorphodon *was about the same size as a large seagull. It had sharp teeth that were used for grabbing wriggling prey. The teeth were unusual, because they had more than one cusp (point). Most pterosaurs had simple, cone-shaped teeth. As* Eudimorphodon *got older, its teeth changed shape. Young ones may have fed on insects, such as dragonflies. Adults may have hunted fish.*

HOW DO I SAY THAT?

● **EUDIMORPHODON**
YOO-DIE-MORF-OH-DON

● **PETEINOSAURUS**
PET-INE-OH-SAW-RUS

FACTFILE: EUDIMORPHODON

Lived: 220 million years ago

Group: Ramphorhynchoidea

Size: 90 cm (3 foot) wingspan

Weight: 600 grams (24 ounces)

Discovery: 1973, Cene, Northern Italy

Diet: insects and fish

Special features: multipointed teeth

Name means: 'true two-form tooth'

FOOD FOR FISH?

A fossil specimen of the Triassic pterosaur, *Preondactylus*, shows that it may have been caught by a huge predatory fish.

When *Preondactylus* was discovered in 1978, paleontologists were surprised to find all the bones squeezed into a tight ball. However, the skeleton was fairly complete, indicating that *Preondactylus* may have been swallowed by a predatory fish. The fish may have later spat out the undigestible bones. These would have sunk to bottom of the sea and fossilized in the bedrock.

Preondactylus was the third-oldest pterosaur to be found, after *Eudimorphodon* and *Peteinosaurus*. The discovery, although it was exciting and rare, did not add to scientists' knowledge about the pterosaurs. It seems that the first pterosaurs were a group of reptiles with well-developed flight features, whose origins remain a mystery. The hunt for their ancestors in older rocks continues.

Caring parent
Preondactylus *was a small pterosaur, about the same size as a pigeon. It had short wings and its jaws were lined with sharp, pointed teeth of different lengths. It is not clear whether* Preondactylus *fed on insects or fish. Like birds today, mothers may have cared for their babies that are too young to fly.*

FACTFILE: PREONDACTYLUS

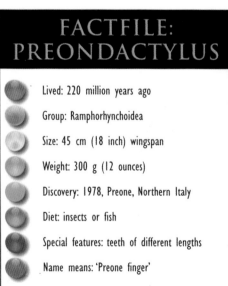

Lived: 220 million years ago

Group: Ramphorhynchoidea

Size: 45 cm (18 inch) wingspan

Weight: 300 g (12 ounces)

Discovery: 1978, Preone, Northern Italy

Diet: insects or fish

Special features: teeth of different lengths

Name means: 'Preone finger'

Unusual end

Did Preondactylus *meet an untimely end? Fossil evidence suggests that the pterosaur was eaten by the huge fish* Saurichthys, *which then spat out the crushed bones.*

Preondactylus

WHERE DID THEY LIVE?

● *Preondactylus*

FISH-EATING PTEROSAURS

Pterosaurs spread all over the world during the Jurassic Period. The earliest Jurassic pterosaur was the long-tailed *Dimorphodon*, a relative of *Peteinosaurus*.

The first *Dimorphodon* fossils were discovered in 1828, on the south coast of England, by the British fossil collector Mary Anning. She is famous for discovering fossils of icthyosaurs and plesiosaurs – giant reptiles that lived in the sea.

Dimorphodon had a relatively large head. The skull was not as heavy as it looked, because it was full of hollow spaces. The sides of the head and beak may have been bright-coloured like puffins and toucans today. *Dimorphodon* had sharp, pointed teeth, which indicates that it was a fish-eater. It might have been hit by a large wave as it was hunting for food.

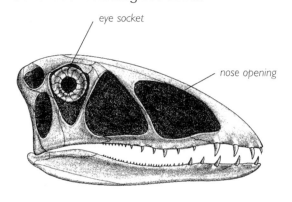

eye socket

nose opening

Big mouth
Dimorphodon had two types of teeth that were used to grab and hold onto slippery fish.

HOW DO I SAY THAT?

● **DIMORPHODON**
DIE-<u>MORF</u>-OH-DON

Steering clear

Dimorphodon *had a long, stiff tail, which may have had a diamond-shaped plate at the end. The tail was probably used as a rudder, to help the pterosaur steer as it flew in gusty winds.* Dimorphodon *had long fingers and claws on its hands. They were probably used to climb over rocks and trees.*

Dimorphodon

FACTFILE: DIMORPHODON

- Lived: 200 million years ago
- Group: Rhamphorhynchoidea
- Size: 90 cm (3 foot) wingspan
- Weight: 1 kg (2 pounds)
- Discovery: 1828, Dorset, England, U.K.
- Diet: fish
- Special features: deep jaws; spaced, sharp teeth
- Name means: 'two-form teeth'

FOSSIL WONDERS

Pterodactylus is probably the best-known pterosaur after which the pterodactyloid group of pterosaurs got their name.

The pterodactyloids dominated the Jurassic skies and probably evolved from the rhamphorhynchoids of the Triassic Period. Many pterosaurs lived in coastal areas or around lakes. They often fell into the water when they died. Some of the best pterosaur fossils, such as those of **Pterodactylus** and *Rhamphorhynchus,* were discovered in the limestone deposits of Solnhofen in Germany. During the Jurassic Period, Solnhofen was covered by a lagoon. This created the perfect environment for fossilizing the remains of pterosaurs.

The fossils of *Rhamphorhynchus* and **Pterodactylus** clearly show the skeleton and imprints of the wing membranes. Their discovery has contributed greatly to our knowledge of pterosaurs. Other fossils have been found on the south coast of England and in Tanzania, Africa.

FACTFILE: PTERODACTYLUS

- Lived: 150 million years ago
- Group: Pterodactyloidea
- Size: 36-250 cm (1-8 foot) wingspan
- Weight: up to 2 kg (4 1/2 pounds)
- Discovery: 1784, Bavaria, Germany
- Diet: fish
- Special features: pointed snout, short tail
- Name means: 'wing-finger'

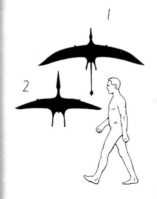

1. *Rhamphorhynchus*
2. *Pterodactylus*

Pterodactylus

Swooping over shallow waters, Pterodactylus *probably snatched fish from the water and returned to land to feed. Fossils show that* Pterodactylus *had a throat pouch similar to that of a pelican, which may have been used to store food.* Pterodactylus *differed from rhamphorhynchoids, such as Rhamphorhynchus. It had a short tail and longer head and neck. Its skull was lighter, and met the neck at a right angle, rather than a straight line.* Pterodactylus *also had longer wrist bones, so its fingers were farther down the wing compared to Rhamphorhynchus.*

HOW DO I SAY THAT?

● PTERODACTYLUS
TER-OH-DAK-TI-LUS

● RHAMPHORHYNCHUS
RAM-FOR-HINE-KUS

Rhamphorhynchus

Dozens of Rhamphorhynchus *fossils have been found. These range from sparrow-sized baby skeletons, to adults as big as an albatross.*

Rhamphorhynchus had a long tail like the early pterosaurs. Its sharp teeth suggest that it was a fish-eater.

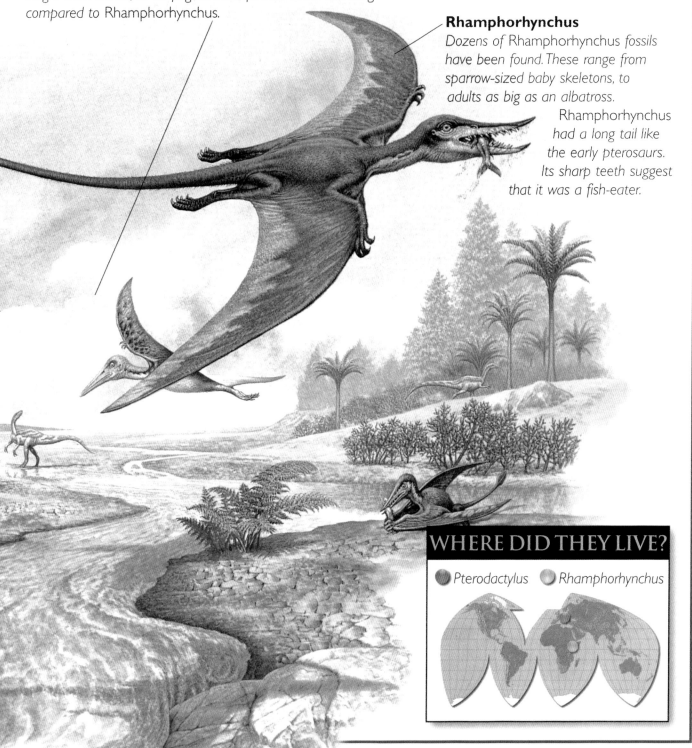

WHERE DID THEY LIVE?

● Pterodactylus   ● Rhamphorhynchus

SHORT-LIVED PTEROSAURS

Above the Jurassic shorelines, the sky teemed with rhamphorhynchoid-type pterosaurs, many of whom died out by the end of this period.

Scaphognathus and *Anurognathus* have been found only in the rocks at Solnhofen in Germany. Along with other long-tailed pterosaurs, they both died out before the end of the Jurassic Period.

   Scaphognathus was similar to *Rhamphorhynchus*. It had long wings and a stiff tail, with a steering plate at the end. However, *Scaphognathus* had a shorter head, a blunt mouth and few teeth. *Anurognathus* was a strange-looking creature that may have been the smallest pterosaur. Its 50 cm (20 inch) wingspan made it the same size as a rook. Only one *Anurognathus* skeleton has been found – a single late Jurassic fossil at Solnhofen.

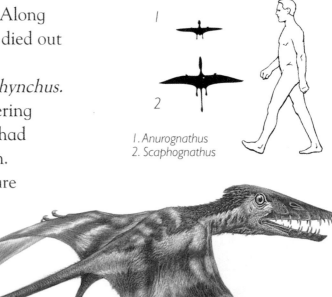

1. Anurognathus
2. Scaphognathus

Scaphognathus
This pterosaur had long, slender wings, so it could fly for long distances. Unlike fish-eating Rhamphorhynchus, *which had forward-sloping teeth, the teeth of* Scaphognathus *pointed upward. It is not certain whether* Scaphognathus *fed on fish or insects.*

Anurognathus

A small pterosaur with a blunt skull and short, peglike teeth, which suggests it ate insects. It must have been an agile, graceful flier to hunt dragonflies and other flying prey. Its tail was unusually short, but other skeletal features make it a rhamphorhynchoid pterosaur, rather than a pterodactyl.

Head

The fossilized skull of Scaphognathus shows that this pterosaur had slender, widely spaced teeth. The small holes around the outside edge of the upper jaw are the sockets for the 18 teeth.

Side view

eye socket

nose opening

Bottom view – upper jaw

teeth sockets

HOW DO I SAY THAT?

ANUROGNATHUS
AN-YOO-ROG-NAY-THUS

SCAPHOGNATHUS
SKAF-OG-NAY-THUS

CREST-HEADS

Some pterodactyloid pterosaurs, such as *Germanodactylus* and *Gallodactylus,* had unusual crests on their heads.

When the fossils of *Gallodactylus* and *Germanodactylus* were discovered at Solnhofen in Germany, scientists thought they were *Pterodactylus* fossils. Both had the physical features of a typical pterodactyloid, such as a short tail. However, when paleontologists studied the skulls more closely, they discovered that these pterosaurs had strange, horny crests on their heads.

Gallodactylus had a point at the back of its head that may have been used for signalling. *Germanodactylus* had a straight crest on the top of its nose. Scientists think that this may have been used as a 'cut-water'. This was a structure that stopped the head from wobbling as the pterosaur dipped into the sea to snatch fish when it hunted for food. Both pterosaurs died out by the end of the Jurassic Period.

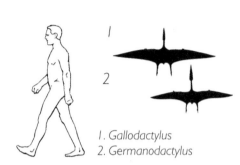

1. *Gallodactylus*
2. *Germanodactylus*

Gallodactylus
A medium-sized pterosaur with a wingspan of 1.35 metres (4 1/2 feet) — *much larger than a seagull.* Gallodactylus *had teeth at the front ends of its long, slender jaws. These pointed forward and would have been used to pluck slippery fish from the water.*

WHERE DID THEY LIVE?

● *Gallodactylus* and *Germanodactylus*

HOW DO I SAY THAT?

● GALLODACTYLUS
GAL-OH-DAK-TIH-LUS

● GERMANODACTYLUS
JER-MAN-OH-DAK-TIH-LUS

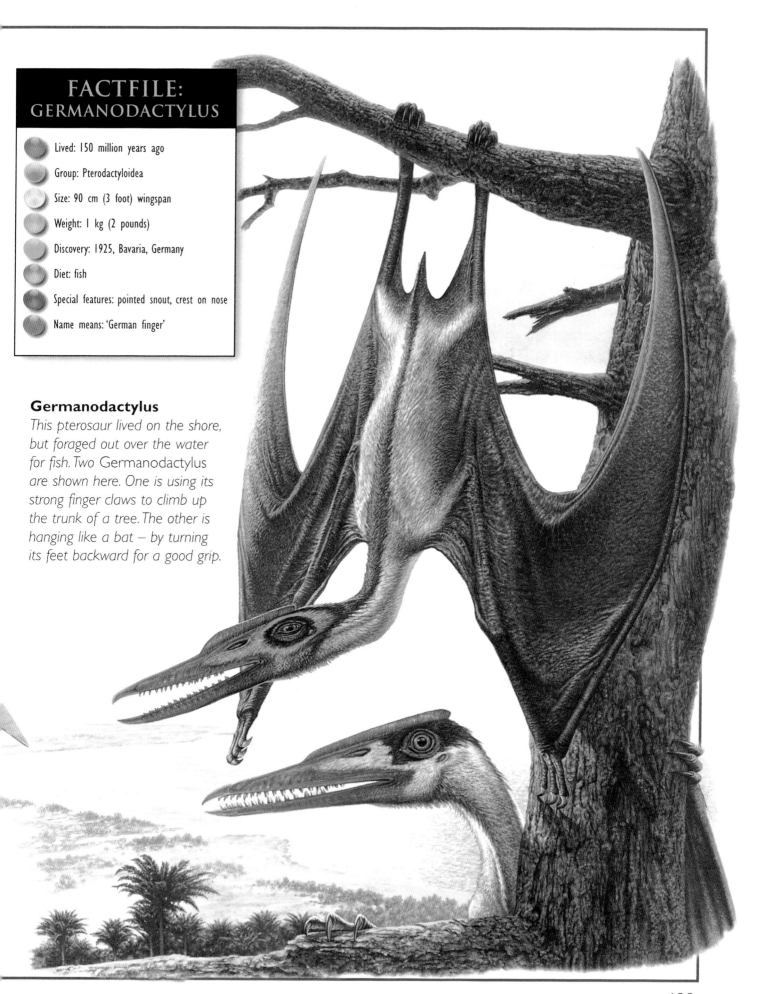

- Lived: 150 million years ago
- Group: Pterodactyloidea
- Size: 90 cm (3 foot) wingspan
- Weight: 1 kg (2 pounds)
- Discovery: 1925, Bavaria, Germany
- Diet: fish
- Special features: pointed snout, crest on nose
- Name means: 'German finger'

Germanodactylus

This pterosaur lived on the shore, but foraged out over the water for fish. Two Germanodactylus are shown here. One is using its strong finger claws to climb up the trunk of a tree. The other is hanging like a bat – by turning its feet backward for a good grip.

FISH-TRAPPERS

Ctenochasma and *Gnathosaurus* were different from most pterosaurs. They had a strange way of feeding, using their jaws to filter fish from the water.

Only two or three fossils of *Ctenochasma* and *Gnathosaurus* were discovered in the limestone rocks of Solnhofen in Germany. Not only are they rare finds, they are also unusual pterodactyloids. They had extraordinary, long heads with a broadened tip at the end of their beaks. The jaws were lined with hundreds of tiny, slender teeth that stuck out sideways like a comb. The teeth formed a trap when they fished for food. These pterosaurs fed by scooping up large mouthfuls of water. When they raised their heads, the water would drain between their teeth. Then they swallowed the sea creatures that were left behind in their mouths.

HOW DO I SAY THAT?
● CTENOCHASMA STEN-OH-CAS-MAH
● GNATHOSAURUS NATH-OH-SAW-RUS

Water filters
Ctenochasma *had over 250 teeth. It probably did not feed in flight but by swimming or wading in the shallow waters of the Solnhofen lagoon and other bodies of water.*

Gnathosaurus

A large pterosaur, with a wingspan of 1.7 metres (5 1/2 feet). When a piece of its jaw was first discovered in 1832, it was mistaken for a crocodile! Gnathosaurus had fewer teeth than Ctenochasma and a more spoon-shaped jaw. It is shown below dipping its head for fish. Another Gnathosaurus flies off in search of food elsewhere.

FACTFILE: CTENOCHASMA

- Lived: 150 million years ago
- Group: Pterodactyloidea
- Size: 1.2 m (4 foot) wingspan
- Weight: 1 kg (2 pounds)
- Discovery: 1851, Saxony, Germany
- Diet: fish
- Special features: broad snout tip and cage of teeth
- Name means: 'comb jaw'

1. Ctenochasma
2. Gnathosaurus

FURRY FLIERS

Fossil evidence shows that the pterosaur *Sordes* was covered with hair.

Fossils normally only show the hard parts of an animal, such as the bones. The softer parts, such as the flesh and skin, usually rot before fossilization takes place. *Sordes* and *Batrachognathus* were found in rocks that were unusual, because they were formed by the fine sediment deposits at the bottom of a lake. Paleontologists had found beautifully preserved fossils of plants and insects before discovering five or six pterosaur skeletons. When paleontologists studied the skeleton of *Sordes* under a microscope, they could clearly see thick hair covering the back and neck, and thinner hair on the wings.

Sordes

Complete fossil
This is a drawing of a fossil of Sordes that was found in the Jurassic deposits of Kazakhstan in Asia. It shows the outline of the wings and thick hair covering the back.

HOW DO I SAY THAT?

● **BATRACHOGNATHUS**
BA-TRACH-OG-NATH-US

● **SORDES**
SOR-DAYS

1. *Sordes*
2. *Batrachognathus*   2

Sordes

This pterosaur was a small, long-tailed rhamphorhynchoid. It may have been a relative of another Jurassic pterosaur, Scaphognathus, discovered in Solnhofen deposits in Germany. Both have a similar head, upright teeth set far apart and relatively short wing fingers.

Batrachognathus

Incomplete fossils of another furry pterosaur – Batrachognathus – were found in the deposits in Kazakhstan. Its physical features suggest it was a close relative of Anurognathus. It had a short tail, broad head and frog-like mouth.

FACTFILE: SORDES

- Lived: 150 million years ago
- Group: Rhamphorhynchoidea
- Size: 60 cm (24 inch) wingspan
- Weight: 500 g (1 pound)
- Discovery: 1970, Kazakhstan, Asia
- Diet: insects
- Special features: broad wings, hair
- Name means: 'devil'

113

WEIRD PTEROSAURS

Pterosaurs became even more varied and spectacular during the Cretaceous Period, which lasted from 150 to 65 million years ago.

The dsungaripterids were the first flying monsters. With wingspans of 3 metres (10 feet), these pterosaurs were as big as today's largest birds – the condor and the albatross. Fossils of skeletons show that these pterosaurs had bizarre-shaped head crests and extraordinary snouts and jaws, which curved upward. The shape of the jaws usually indicates how an animal lived and what it ate. *Dsungaripterus* had jaws lined with blunt, bony knobs instead of teeth. The narrow, pointed jaws may have been used to prize shellfish from rocky crannies. Shells would have been crushed by the bony knobs in the mouth.

Fantastic head crests

Crests allowed pterosaurs to signal to each other and to identify members of their own species. Some pterosaurs may have had crests to help them steer in the sky or through water.

WHERE DID THEY LIVE?

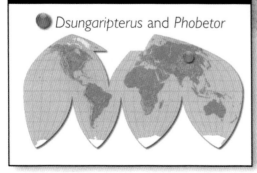

● *Dsungaripterus* and *Phobetor*

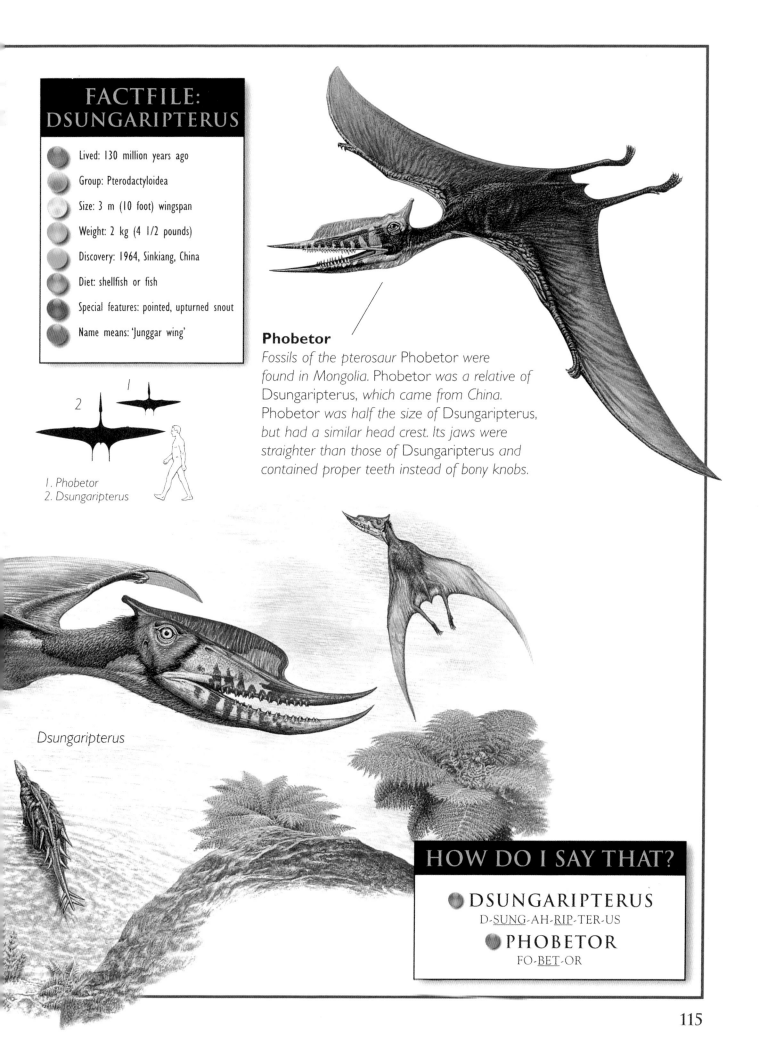

FACTFILE: DSUNGARIPTERUS

- Lived: 130 million years ago
- Group: Pterodactyloidea
- Size: 3 m (10 foot) wingspan
- Weight: 2 kg (4 1/2 pounds)
- Discovery: 1964, Sinkiang, China
- Diet: shellfish or fish
- Special features: pointed, upturned snout
- Name means: 'Junggar wing'

1
2

1. Phobetor
2. Dsungaripterus

Phobetor

Fossils of the pterosaur Phobetor *were found in Mongolia.* Phobetor *was a relative of* Dsungaripterus, *which came from China.* Phobetor *was half the size of* Dsungaripterus, *but had a similar head crest. Its jaws were straighter than those of* Dsungaripterus *and contained proper teeth instead of bony knobs.*

Dsungaripterus

HOW DO I SAY THAT?

● DSUNGARIPTERUS
D-SUNG-AH-RIP-TER-US

● PHOBETOR
FO-BET-OR

115

FILTER-FEEDERS

Pterodaustro fed like a blue whale does today – its huge jaws filtered tiny creatures from the water.

Pterodaustro had an amazing set of flexible teeth in its lower jaw – more than 2,000 of them. The teeth worked like a fishing net. The pterosaur dipped its jaw into the lake and skimmed along the surface of the water. Fish, shrimp and other water creatures were trapped in the teeth and then swallowed. This is similar to the way blue whales feed today. Earlier pterosaurs, such as _Gnathosaurus_ and _Ctenochasma_ of the Jurassic Period, may have filtered their food in this way, too. However, they did not have quite as many teeth as _Pterodaustro_.

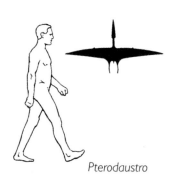

Pterodaustro

Big differences
Pterodaustro _has been called the 'flamingo pterosaur' by scientists, because it had a very long head compared to the length of its body._

WHERE DID THEY LIVE?

🔴 *Pterodaustro*

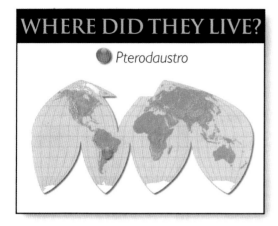

Weird teeth

These pictures of the head of Pterodaustro show its amazing teeth. When the jaws were shut, the lower teeth would stick out above the snout. The lower jaw had long, elastic bristles for teeth to filter tiny creatures from the water. The upper jaw had small, blunt teeth to chop up food.

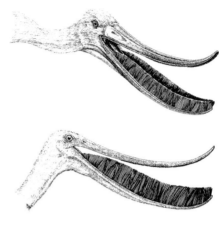

FACTFILE: PTERODAUSTRO

- Lived: 140 million years ago
- Group: Pterodactyloidea
- Size: 1.3 m (4 foot) wingspan
- Weight: 3 kg (6 1/2 pounds)
- Discovery: 1970, Argentina
- Diet: small fish and other sea creatures
- Special features: 2,000 flexible, long teeth
- Name means: 'southern wing'

Feeding

Pterodaustro squats and dips its lower jaw into the water to trap little creatures that float near the surface. This pterosaur may have skimmed for food by swinging its head from side to side, to drain water through its lower teeth.

HOW DO I SAY THAT?

🔴 PTERODAUSTRO
TERO-<u>DAW</u>-STRO

FLYING GIANTS

Among the largest pterosaurs were *Pteranodon* and *Nyctosaurus*. They were almost as big as a small aeroplane!

When the first fossils of *Pteranodon* were found in North America in 1870, paleontologists were amazed at their size. All they had found was a bone from the hand, but they could see it was ten times the size of the same hand bone in a *Pterodactylus* skeleton. Paleontologists thought that the bone came from a pterosaur with a wingspan of at least 6 metres (20 feet). More complete fossils of *Pteranodon* have now been found. These fossils indicate that the pterosaur had a bony crest at the back of its skull and no teeth in its mouth. *Nyctosaurus* was a smaller, toothless pterosaur from the same area as *Pteranodon*. It had a much shorter crest at the back of its head.

In late Cretaceous times, several species of *Pteranodon* and *Nyctosaurus* lived over a shallow sea that covered the middle of what is now the USA. The outstretched wingspan of the largest species was 9 metres (30 feet). This is bigger than any living bird and would have been as long as a bus!

HOW DO I SAY THAT?

● **NYCTOSAURUS**
NIK-TOE-SAW-RUS

● **PTERANODON**
TER-AN-OH-DON

1. *Nyctosaurus*
2. *Pteranodon*

WHERE DID THEY LIVE?

● *Nyctosaurus* and *Pteranodon*

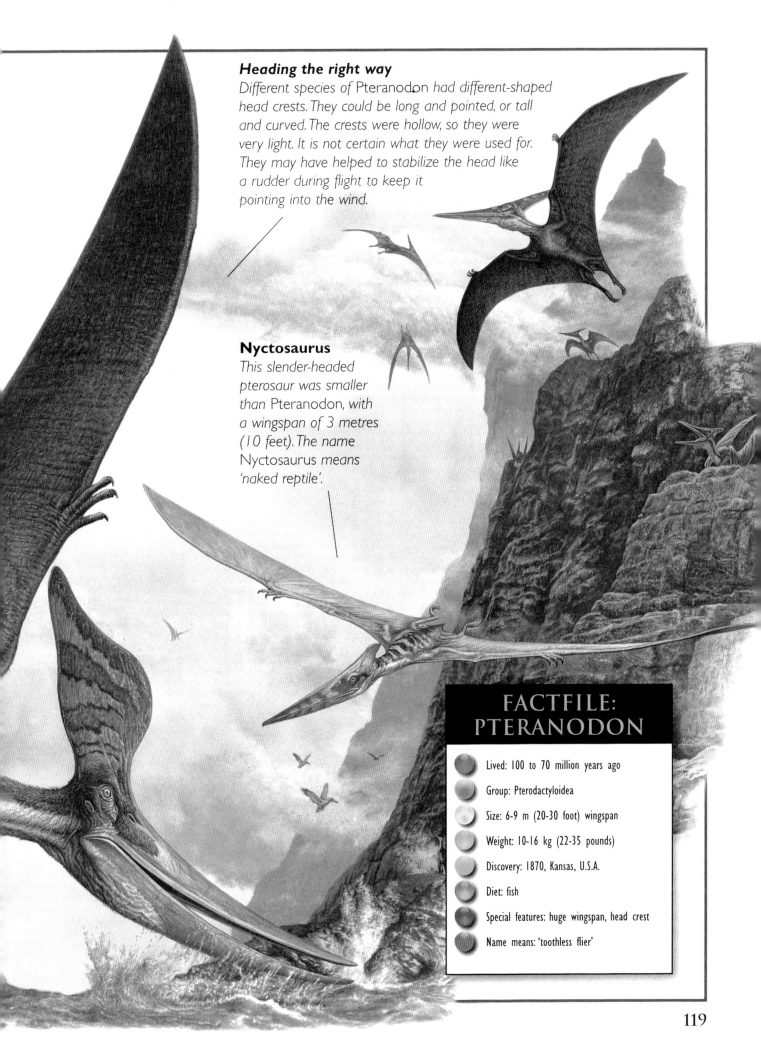

Heading the right way

Different species of Pteranodon *had different-shaped head crests. They could be long and pointed, or tall and curved. The crests were hollow, so they were very light. It is not certain what they were used for. They may have helped to stabilize the head like a rudder during flight to keep it pointing into the wind.*

Nyctosaurus

This slender-headed pterosaur was smaller than Pteranodon, *with a wingspan of 3 metres (10 feet). The name* Nyctosaurus *means 'naked reptile'.*

FACTFILE: PTERANODON

Lived: 100 to 70 million years ago

Group: Pterodactyloidea

Size: 6-9 m (20-30 foot) wingspan

Weight: 10-16 kg (22-35 pounds)

Discovery: 1870, Kansas, U.S.A.

Diet: fish

Special features: huge wingspan, head crest

Name means: 'toothless flier'

WINGED MONSTER

Pteranodon **was believed to be the largest flying animal ever –
until 1971, when an even larger pterosaur fossil was discovered.**

Quetzalcoatlus was found on the 'big bend' of the Rio Grande river. The
'Texas pterosaur', as it was called, was a true flying monster. With a wingspan
of 40 feet (12 metres), it was twice as big as *Pteranodon.* It had a head crest
and no teeth. Unlike *Pteranodon,* it had slender jaws that ended in a
long, narrow, pointed beak and an extremely long, rigid neck.

The discovery excited scientists. *Quetzalcoatlus* was not
only the largest pterosaur to be found, it was also the
last of the pterosaurs to live on earth. It survived
to the end of the Cretaceous Period,
65 million years ago, when all the
pterosaurs and dinosaurs
suddenly died out.

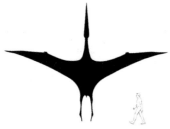

Quetzalcoatlus

Quetzalcoatlus
*This pterosaur had such huge wings that
they would have broken if they flapped
too fast. Quetzalcoatlus probably glided
on warm air currents, moving its wings
slightly to adjust its position.*

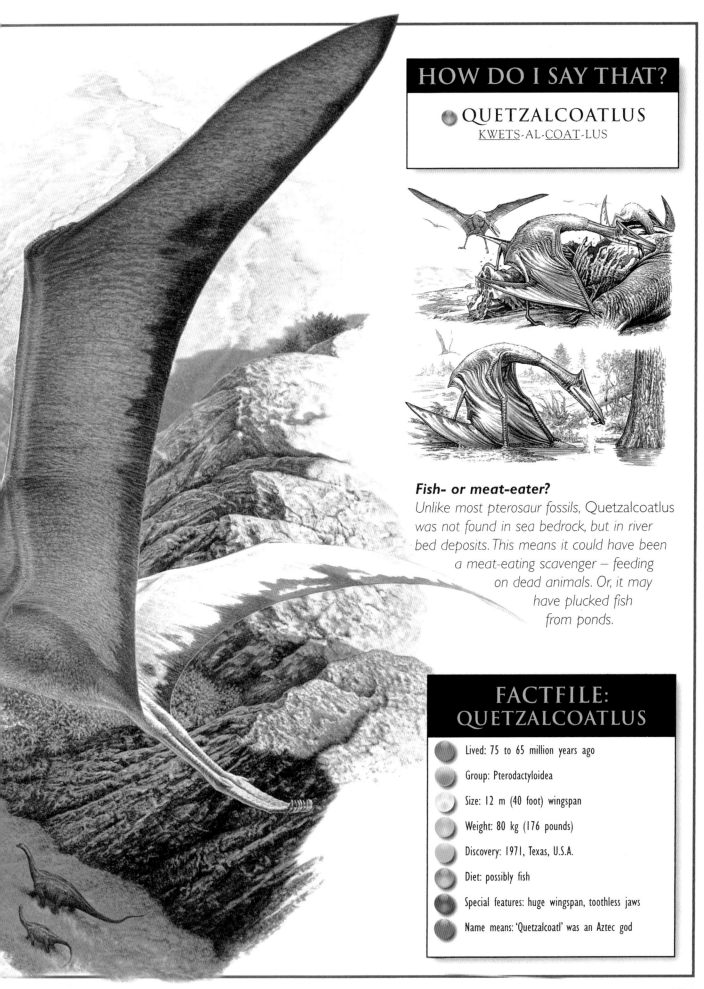

Fish- or meat-eater?

Unlike most pterosaur fossils, Quetzalcoatlus was not found in sea bedrock, but in river bed deposits. This means it could have been a meat-eating scavenger – feeding on dead animals. Or, it may have plucked fish from ponds.

FACTFILE: QUETZALCOATLUS

Lived: 75 to 65 million years ago

Group: Pterodactyloidea

Size: 12 m (40 foot) wingspan

Weight: 80 kg (176 pounds)

Discovery: 1971, Texas, U.S.A.

Diet: possibly fish

Special features: huge wingspan, toothless jaws

Name means: 'Quetzalcoatl' was an Aztec god

INDEX

INDEX